SOUP RECIPES

100 Simple and Delicious Soup Maker Recipes for a Healthy Life

Inna Volia

Table of Contents

INTRODUCTION 5
Soup Benefits: 6
Some tips on how to use your soup maker: 7
1-Squash Leek Soup 8
2-Pepper & Sweet Potato Soup 10
3-Potato Leek Soup 12
4-Roasted Tomato Veggie Soup 14
5-Carrot Soup 16
6-Delicious Cauliflower Curried Soup 18
7-Winter Vegetable Soup 20
8-Yellow Lentil Soup 22
9-Tasty Carrot Spinach Soup 24
10-Parsnip Soup 26
11-Vegetable Tomato Soup 28
12-Creamy Mushroom Soup 30
13-Garlic Mushroom Soup 32
14-Onion Asparagus Soup 34
15-Thyme Asparagus Soup 36
16-Ginger Carrot Soup 38
17-Apple Potato Leek Soup 40
18-Moroccan Carrot Soup 42
19-Mixed Vegetable Soup 44
20-Delicious Sweet Corn Soup 46
21-Flavours Mediterranean Veggie Soup 48
22-Easy Tomato Pepper Soup 50
23-Yummy Chicken Noodle Soup 52
24-Mix Herbed Potato Leek Soup 54
25-Spicy Chili Pepper Soup 56
26-Root Vegetable Soup 58
27-Spicy Potato Squash Soup 60
28-Simple Swede Soup 62
29-Pea Mint Soup 64
30-Healthy Pea Soup 66
31-Pea Leek Soup 68
32-Pea Ham Soup 70
33-Healthy Green Soup 72
34-Easy Pumpkin Soup 74

35-Cheddar Broccoli Soup 76
36-Flavorful Broccoli Soup 78
37-Simple Carrot Broccoli Soup 80
38-Simple Cauliflower Broccoli Soup 82
39-Winter Vegetable Soup 84
40-Black Bean Potato Soup 86
41-Apple Carrot Soup 88
42-Sweet Squash Apple Soup 90
43-Creamy Parsnip Apple Soup 92
44-Apple Cauliflower Soup 94
45-Simple Apple Parsnip Soup 96
46-Tasty Red Lentil Soup 98
47-Lentil Vegetable Soup 100
48-Red Lentil Sweet Potato Soup 102
49-Chunky Squash Soup 104
50-Delicious Cauliflower Curried Soup 106
51-Yummy Chicken Chorizo Soup 108
52-Onion Cheese Soup 110
53-Roasted Pepper Soup 112
54-Chickpea Cabbage Soup 114
55-Healthy Kale Soup 116
56-Lentil Tomato Soup 118
57-Vegan Lentil Soup 120
58-Spicy Lentil Carrot Soup 122
59-Beetroot Soup 124
60-Orange Carrot Beetroot Soup 126
61-Prawn Soup 128
62-Tofu Prawn Soup 130
63-Delicious Fish Soup 132
64-Salmon Soup 134
65-Beef Soup 136
66-Tasty Mexican Soup 138
67-Spicy Kidney Bean Soup 140
68-Easy Chili Sweet Potato Soup 142
69-Flavorful Potato Soup 144
70-Simple Chicken Corn Soup 146
71-Mushroom Chicken Soup 148
72-Creamy Zucchini Soup 150
73-Zucchini Carrot Potato Soup 152

74-Easy Cauliflower Soup 154
75-Anti-inflammatory Broccoli Ginger Soup......................... 156
76-Lime Asparagus Cauliflower Soup................................... 158
77-Flavorful Asparagus Soup 160
78-Spinach Broccoli Soup 162
79-Healthy Bean Soup 164
80-Smooth Berry Apple Soup 166
81-Creamy Lentil Soup.. 168
82-Basil Tomato Soup..170
83-Thai Chicken Soup..172
84-Bell Pepper Tomato Soup 174
85-Spinach Coconut Soup..176
86-Almond Broccoli Soup 178
87-Beef Mushroom Soup 180
88-Chunky Onion Soup 182
89-Potato Chickpea Soup... 184
90-Creamy Potato Leek Soup 186
91-Paprika Pumpkin Soup 188
92-Autumn Bean Soup.. 190
93-Avocado Zucchini Soup 192
94-Green Bean Tomato Soup.. 194
95-Celery Soup 196
96-Chunky Veggie Soup... 198
97-Eggplant Asparagus Soup...200
98-Creamy Eggplant Soup...202
99-Sweetcorn Chicken Soup 204
100-Chunky Zucchini Bean Soup 206
Conclusion:..208

INTRODUCTION

A flavorful bowl of soup fills you up, reduces cravings and keeps you energized for hours. Soup is something familiar to everyone. Soup means so many things to so many people for good reason. In a word Soup means comfort. In more words, it means, "Home. Satisfaction. Nutritious"

Soup is nutritious and easy to incorporate into your daily diet. It can be low in calories if you are on a calorie controlled diet plan. Some people think soups are just for the colder months but they are totally wrong. It can be a refreshing and vibrant alternative on the hottest and brightest of days, and make use of the best seasonal ingredients all year around. You can enjoy soup year around.

Soups made from nutrient-rich vegetables. Eating a bowl of soup is one way of having your daily recommended serving of vegetables and fruits. Raw vegetables and fruits are not appealing to our taste. Making them into soups improves their taste and makes them easier to eat. Eating a bowl of vegetable soup before the main meal helps you eat less. It has been proven that soups can help to lose and maintain a healthy weight.

Soup maker is a wonderful kitchen appliance for soup lovers it simplifies soup making. You just need easy and delicious recipes like the ones found in this book. Soup making is so simple after preparing ingredients, you place them in the soup maker, close the lid, and select smooth, chunky, blend mode. Yes, that is how easy it is.

Try all the recipes in this book and share your favorite ones with family, friends, and colleagues.

Happy souping!

Soup Benefits:

- Highly nutritious: Soup is known to be highly nutritious because of the variety of possible ingredient combinations, including vegetables, herbs, grains, spices, meat, and fruits.
- Easy and economical: Soup is not only easy to prepare and tasty, it can be economical as well.
- Energy booster: Because of the combination of carbohydrates, proteins, and other nutrients, as well as easy digestibility of soup, it gives a steady supply of energy to our bodies.

Some tips on how to use your soup maker:

- Keep ready all your ingredients first.
- Do not use raw meat, only use cooked meat.
- Use only boneless meat in the soup maker.
- Cut your ingredients into small chunks before adding to the soup maker.
- Always use hot stock in recipes.
- Always make sure the soup maker lid is tightly sealed and fastened before cooking.
- Follow the manufacturer's instructions when using the appliance.
- Do not overfill your soup maker. Pay careful attention to the capacity of your soup maker and the fill level markers.

1-Squash Leek Soup

Time: 35 minutes

Serve: 4

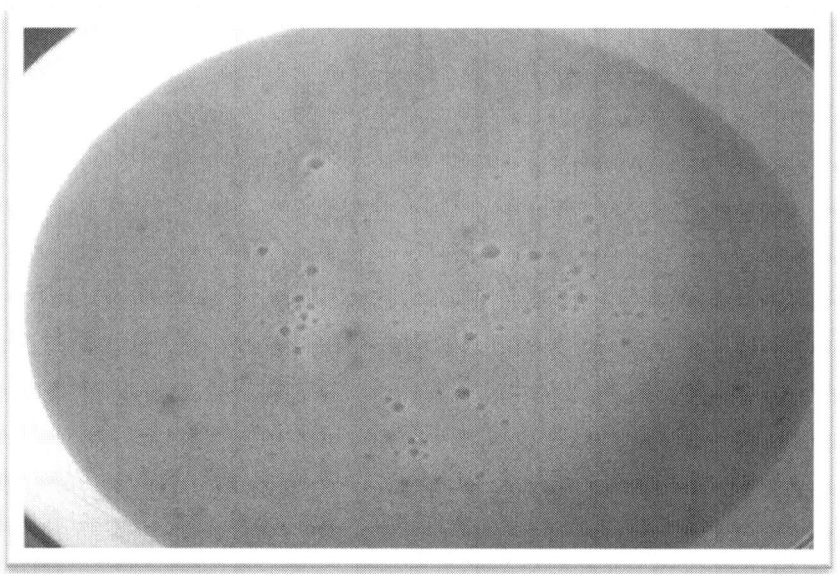

Ingredients:

- 1 large butternut squash, peeled and diced
- 3 tbsp yogurt
- 1 tsp chives
- 1 tsp mixed herbs
- 1 tsp garlic paste
- 1 cup water
- 1 large onion, diced
- 4 leeks, chopped
- Pepper
- Salt

Directions:

- Add onion, leeks, and squash into the soup maker.
- Add chives, mixed herbs, garlic paste, and water and cook for 25 minutes on the cook and blend mode.
- Once 25 minutes over then add yogurt and blend again.
- Season with pepper and salt.
- Serve warm and enjoy.

Nutritional Value (Amount per Serving):

- Calories 122
- Fat 0.6 g
- Carbohydrates 28.5 g
- Sugar 5.9 g
- Protein 3.3 g
- Cholesterol 1 mg

2-Pepper & Sweet Potato Soup

Time: 35 minutes

Serve: 4

Ingredients:

- 3 red bell peppers, diced
- 1 tsp cumin seeds
- 2 tsp paprika
- 2 garlic cloves
- 1 red chili, chopped
- 1 large onion, diced
- 4 sweet potatoes, peeled and diced
- 2 cups vegetable stock
- 1 tbsp olive oil
- Pepper
- Salt

Directions:

- Heat olive oil in a pan over medium heat.
- Once the oil is hot, add cumin, paprika, onion, sweet potato, and red pepper. Sauté for 5 minutes over medium-high heat.
- Transfer sautéed vegetables to the soup maker. Add remaining ingredients to the soup maker and cook for 20 minutes on cook and blend mode.
- Season with pepper and salt.
- Serve hot and enjoy.

Nutritional Value (Amount per Serving):

- Calories 198
- Fat 5.1 g
- Carbohydrates 38.8 g
- Sugar 12.7 g
- Protein 3.7 g
- Cholesterol 0 mg

3-Potato Leek Soup

Time: 35 minutes

Serve: 4

Ingredients:

- 1 large leek, diced
- 1 tbsp rosemary
- 1/2 cup yogurt
- 2 garlic cloves, chopped
- 3 large potatoes, peeled and diced
- Pepper
- Salt

Directions:

- Add all ingredients except yogurt into the soup maker and stir well.
- Seal soup maker with lid and cook on chunky mode for 28 minutes.
- Add yogurt and cover again and blend well.
- Season with pepper and salt.
- Serve warm and enjoy.

Nutritional Value (Amount per Serving):

- Calories 231
- Fat 0.9 g
- Carbohydrates 49.8 g
- Sugar 6.2 g
- Protein 6.9 g
- Cholesterol 2 mg

4-Roasted Tomato Veggie Soup

Time: 35 minutes

Serve: 4

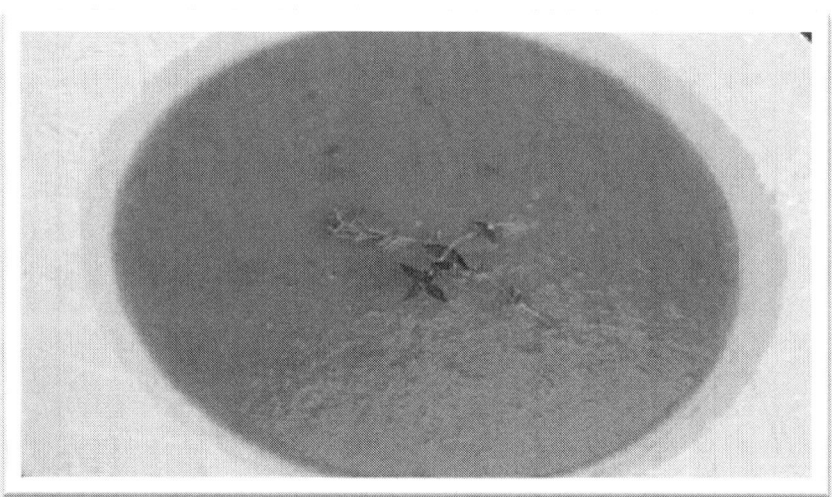

Ingredients:

- 14 tomatoes, roasted in the oven
- 1 garlic clove, roasted
- 6 basil leaves
- ½ bottle gourd, chopped
- 1 cup spinach, chopped
- 1 carrot, peeled and chopped
- 1 beetroot, roasted and chopped
- 1 ½ cups water
- Pepper
- Salt

Directions:

- Add all ingredients to the soup maker and stir well.
- Cover soup maker with lid and cook on smooth mode for 23 minutes.
- Season with pepper and salt.
- Serve and enjoy.

Nutritional Value (Amount per Serving):

- Calories 107
- Fat 1 g
- Carbohydrates 23.6 g
- Sugar 14.1 g
- Protein 5.1 g
- Cholesterol 0 mg

5-Carrot Soup

Time: 35 minutes

Serve: 4

Ingredients:

- 4 cups water
- 1 tsp mix herbs
- 3 chicken stock cubes
- 1 tbsp coriander powder
- 3 large carrots, peeled and chopped
- 1 garlic clove, minced
- 1 small potato, peeled and diced
- 1 tbsp olive oil
- 1 onion, diced
- Pepper
- Salt

Directions:

- Heat oil in a pan over medium heat.
- Add garlic and onion to the pan and sauté until softened.
- Add remaining vegetables and sauté for 5 minutes.
- Add coriander powder and sauté for a minute.
- Transfer sautéed vegetables to the soup maker along with remaining ingredients and stir well.
- Cover soup maker with lid and cook for 20 minutes on smooth mode.
- Season with pepper and salt.
- Serve warm and enjoy.

Nutritional Value (Amount per Serving):

- Calories 104
- Fat 3.7 g
- Carbohydrates 16.4 g
- Sugar 4.2 g
- Protein 2.2 g
- Cholesterol 0 mg

6-Delicious Cauliflower Curried Soup

Time: 35 minutes

Serve: 4

Ingredients:

- 1 large cauliflower head, cut into florets
- 2 chicken stock cubes
- 5 cups of water
- 1 tsp mix herbs
- 1 tsp garam masala
- 1 tsp coriander powder
- ½ tsp ground cumin
- 1 tsp turmeric
- 1 sweet potato, peeled and diced
- 1 tbsp ginger, grated
- 2 garlic cloves, minced

- 1 large onion, diced
- 1 tbsp olive oil
- Pepper
- Salt

Directions:

- Heat oil in a pan over medium heat.
- Add garlic and onion and sauté until tender.
- Add spices and sweet potato and sauté for 2 minutes.
- Transfer sautéed vegetables to the soup maker along with remaining ingredients.
- Cover soup maker with lid and cook for 20 minutes on smooth mode.
- Season with pepper and salt.
- Serve warm and enjoy.

Nutritional Value (Amount per Serving):

- Calories 138
- Fat 4.1 g
- Carbohydrates 23.1 g
- Sugar 8.6 g
- Protein 5.8 g
- Cholesterol 0 mg

7-Winter Vegetable Soup

Time: 35 minutes

Serve: 4

Ingredients:

- 4 cups vegetable stock
- 1 tbsp butter
- 2 baby potato, peeled and washed
- 1 cup turnip, chopped
- 1 cup carrot, sliced
- 1 cup leek, chopped
- 1 large onion, sliced
- Pepper
- Salt

Directions:

- Melt butter in a pan over medium heat.
- Add leek and onion to the pan and sauté until softened.
- Transfer sautéed onion and leek to the soup maker.
- Add remaining ingredients to the soup maker.
- Cover soup maker with lid and cook on smooth mode for 25 minutes.
- Season with pepper and salt.
- Serve hot with bread and enjoy.

Nutritional Value (Amount per Serving):

- Calories 127
- Fat 3.5 g
- Carbohydrates 24.9 g
- Sugar 7.1 g
- Protein 3.3 g
- Cholesterol 8 mg

8-Yellow Lentil Soup

Time: 30 minutes

Serve: 4

Ingredients:

- 1 cup yellow split lentils, soaked and drained
- ¼ tsp ginger garlic paste
- ½ tsp turmeric powder
- ½ tsp chili powder
- 1 onion, diced
- 1 cup carrots, diced
- 1 cup tomatoes, diced
- 1 tsp salt

Directions:

- Add all ingredients to the soup maker and stir well.
- Now add water to the minimum mark.
- Cover soup maker with lid and cook on smooth mode.
- Season with pepper and salt.
- Garnish with cream and serve.

Nutritional Value (Amount per Serving):

- Calories 186
- Fat 0.7 g
- Carbohydrates 32.6 g
- Sugar 3.7 g
- Protein 13.1 g
- Cholesterol 0 mg

9-Tasty Carrot Spinach Soup

Time: 25 minutes

Serve: 2

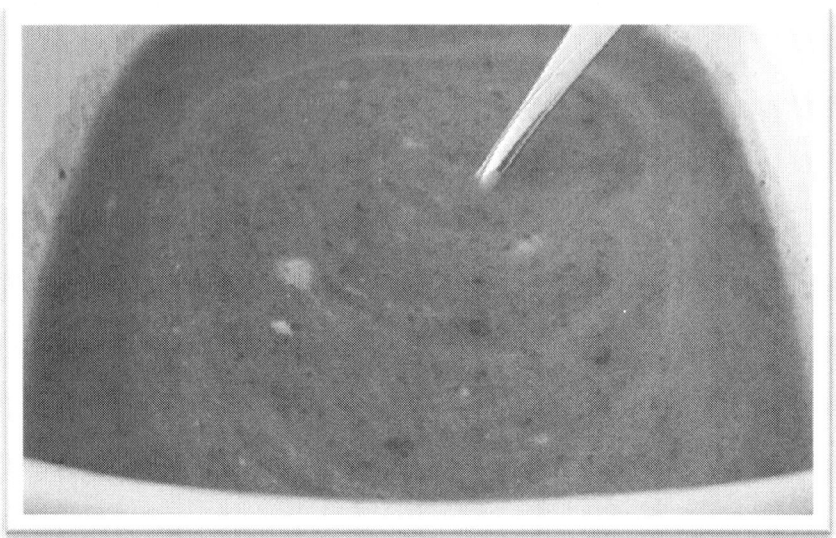

Ingredients:

- 1 cup spinach
- 2 dry chilies
- 1 medium onion, chopped
- 1 tbsp cheddar cheese
- 2 ½ cups of water
- 3 garlic cloves
- 2 carrots, chopped
- Pepper
- Salt

Directions:

- Add all ingredients to the soup maker and mix well.
- Cover soup maker with lid and cook on blend mode.
- Season with pepper and salt.
- Serve warm and enjoy.

Nutritional Value (Amount per Serving):

- Calories 72
- Fat 1.3 g
- Carbohydrates 13.3 g
- Sugar 5.5 g
- Protein 2.7 g
- Cholesterol 4 mg

10-Parsnip Soup

Time: 40 minutes

Serve: 4

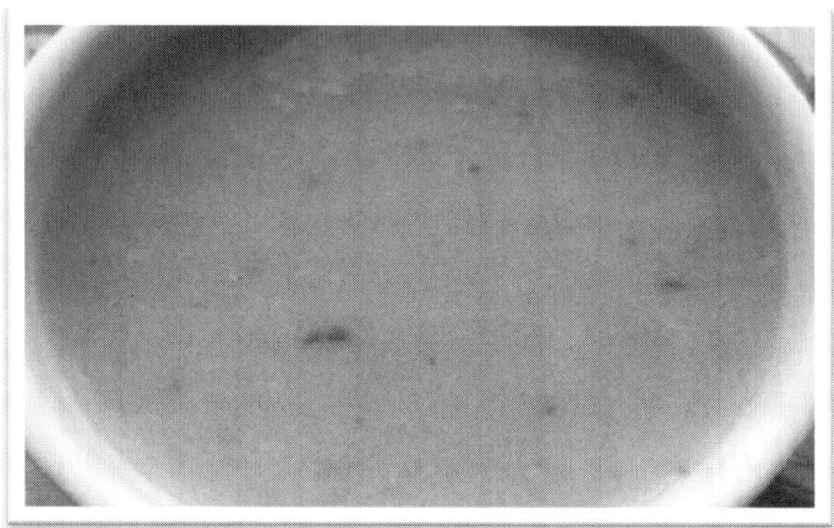

Ingredients:

- 13 oz parsnips
- 4 ½ cups vegetable stock
- 1 tbsp ginger, grated
- 2 garlic cloves
- 1 large onion, chopped
- ½ tsp mustard seeds
- ½ tsp turmeric
- 1 tsp cumin seeds
- 1 tsp coriander seeds
- 2 tbsp olive oil

Directions:

- Heat oil in a pan over medium heat.
- Once the oil is hot then add cumin seeds and mustard seeds and sauté for 30 seconds.
- Add ginger, garlic, spices, and onion and sauté until onion is softened.
- Add parsnips and cook for 5 minutes.
- Transfer sautéed onion mixture to the soup maker.
- Add remaining ingredients to the soup maker.
- Cover soup maker with lid and cook on smooth mode.
- Serve warm and enjoy.

Nutritional Value (Amount per Serving):

- Calories 167
- Fat 9.9 g
- Carbohydrates 24.3 g
- Sugar 8.4 g
- Protein 2 g
- Cholesterol 0 mg

11-Vegetable Tomato Soup

Time: 30 minutes

Serve: 4

Ingredients:

- 28 oz tomatoes, chopped
- 2 cups cherry tomatoes, chopped
- 2 vegetable bouillon cubes
- 2 tbsp olive oil
- ½ cup peas
- 1 leek, chopped
- 1 onion, chopped
- Water
- Pepper
- Salt

Directions:

- Add all ingredients to the soup maker and stir well.
- Add water up to the top line. Cover soup maker with lid and cook on smooth mode.
- Season with pepper and salt.
- Serve hot and enjoy.

Nutritional Value (Amount per Serving):

- Calories 156
- Fat 7.9 g
- Carbohydrates 20 g
- Sugar 11 g
- Protein 4.4 g
- Cholesterol 0 mg

12-Creamy Mushroom Soup

Time: 30 minutes

Serve: 4

Ingredients:

- 1 lb mushrooms, clean and chopped
- 4 cups vegetable stock
- 1 large onion, chopped
- Pepper
- Salt

Directions:

- Add all ingredients to the soup maker.
- Cover soup maker with lid and cook on smooth mode.
- Season with pepper and salt.
- Garnish with chopped chives and serve.

Nutritional Value (Amount per Serving):

- Calories 49
- Fat 2.4 g
- Carbohydrates 9.3 g
- Sugar 5.5 g
- Protein 4 g
- Cholesterol 0 mg

13-Garlic Mushroom Soup

Time: 35 minutes

Serve: 4

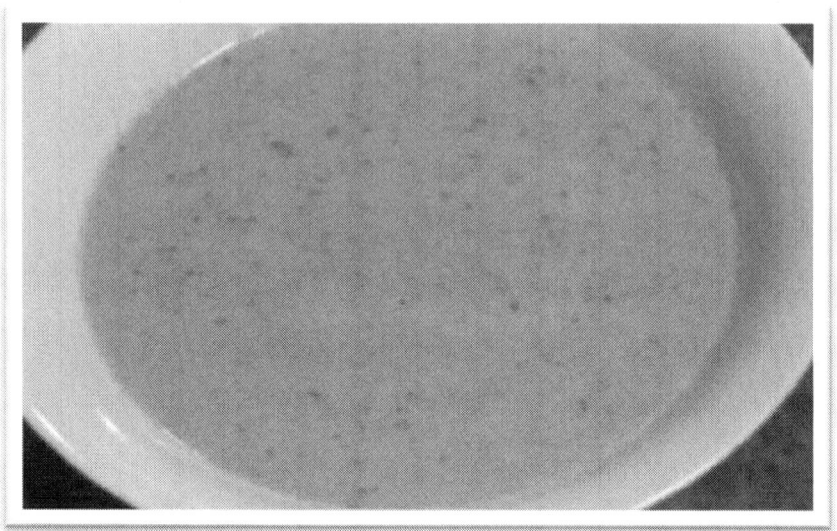

Ingredients:

- 10 mushrooms, chopped
- 1 tbsp butter
- 2 tsp cornflour, dissolve in water
- 1 tsp mix herbs
- 1 potato
- 4 cups chicken stock
- 2 garlic cloves, chopped
- 1 large onion, chopped
- Pepper
- Salt

Directions:

- Add all ingredients to the soup maker and stir well.
- Cover soup maker with lid and cook on smooth mode.
- Season with pepper and salt.
- Serve warm and enjoy.

Nutritional Value (Amount per Serving):

- Calories 99
- Fat 3.7 g
- Carbohydrates 14.6 g
- Sugar 3.4 g
- Protein 3.6 g
- Cholesterol 8 mg

14-Onion Asparagus Soup

Time: 40 minutes

Serve: 6

Ingredients:

- ½ lb asparagus, chopped
- 2 ¾ cups hot water
- 2 chicken stock cubes
- 1 tsp butter
- 1 large potato, cubed
- 1 medium onion, chopped
- ¼ cup spring onion, chopped
- Pepper
- Salt

Directions:

- Melt butter in a pan over medium heat.
- Add spring onion and onion to the pan and sauté until softened.
- Add asparagus and stir well.
- Transfer sautéed onion mixture to the soup maker.
- Add remaining ingredients and stir well.
- Cover soup maker with lid and cook on smooth mode.
- Serve warm and enjoy.

Nutritional Value (Amount per Serving):

- Calories 72
- Fat 0.9 g
- Carbohydrates 14.6 g
- Sugar 2.1 g
- Protein 2.6 g
- Cholesterol 2 mg

15-Thyme Asparagus Soup

Time: 35 minutes

Serve: 4

Ingredients:

- 1 lb asparagus spears, chopped
- 1 tbsp olive oil
- 1 tbsp fresh thyme leaves
- 1 onion, chopped
- 2 ½ cups vegetable stock
- Pepper
- Salt

Directions:

- Heat oil in a pan over medium heat.
- Add onion and sauté until softened.
- Add asparagus and thyme and sauté for 2 minutes.
- Transfer pan mixture to the soup maker.
- Add remaining ingredients to the soup maker.
- Cover soup maker with lid and cook on smooth mode.
- Season with pepper and salt.
- Serve warm and enjoy.

Nutritional Value (Amount per Serving):

- Calories 68
- Fat 4.2 g
- Carbohydrates 7.9 g
- Sugar 3.8 g
- Protein 2.9 g
- Cholesterol 0 mg

16-Ginger Carrot Soup

Time: 30 minutes

Serve: 4

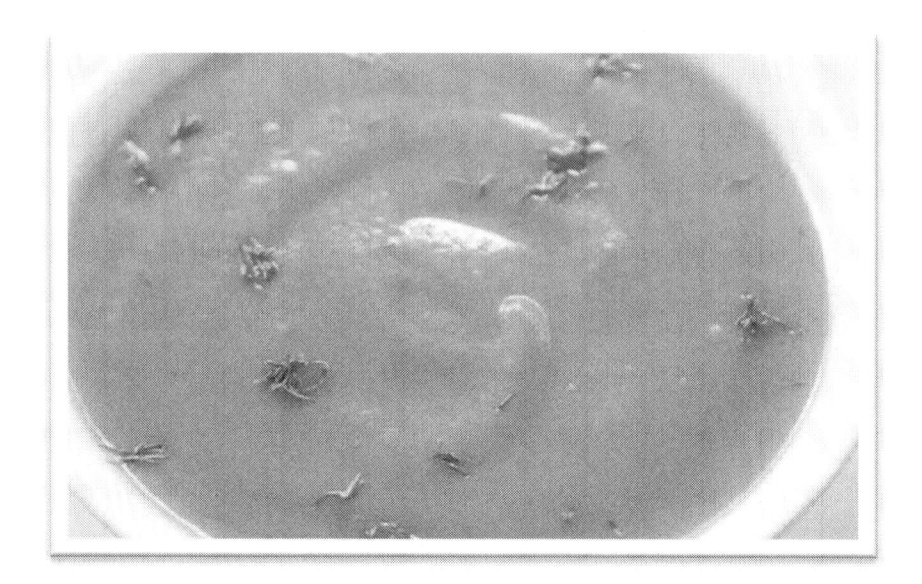

Ingredients:

- 1 lb carrots, peeled and chopped
- 4 cups vegetable stock
- 1 tbsp ginger, grated
- 1 large onion, peeled and chopped
- 1 tbsp olive oil
- ¼ tsp ground black pepper
- 1 tsp salt

Directions:

- Heat olive oil in a pan over medium heat.
- Once the oil is hot then add ginger and onion and sauté until onion is softened.
- Add carrots and sauté for 2 minutes.
- Transfer sautéed onion mixture to the soup maker.
- Add remaining ingredients to the soup maker.
- Cover soup maker with lid and cook on smooth mode.
- Serve warm and enjoy.

Nutritional Value (Amount per Serving):

- Calories 106
- Fat 5.6 g
- Carbohydrates 17.7 g
- Sugar 9.2 g
- Protein 1.5 g
- Cholesterol 0 mg

17-Apple Potato Leek Soup

Time: 30 minutes

Serve: 4

Ingredients:

- 2/3 cup coconut milk
- 1 garlic clove, crushed
- 2 vegetable stock cubes
- 1 tbsp olive oil
- 2 oz asparagus spears
- 1 ½ apple, peeled and chopped
- 2 medium potatoes, peeled and chopped
- 1 ¼ cups leek, chopped
- 1 tsp salt
- Water

Directions:

- Heat olive oil in a pan over medium heat.
- Add garlic, onion, and leek to the pan and sauté until leek is softened.
- Transfer pan mixture to the soup maker.
- Add remaining ingredients to the soup maker and stir well.
- Add water to the soup maker until the maximum level.
- Cover soup maker with lid and cook on smooth mode.
- Serve warm and enjoy.

Nutritional Value (Amount per Serving):

- Calories 265
- Fat 13.6 g
- Carbohydrates 35.8 g
- Sugar 12.6 g
- Protein 3.9 g
- Cholesterol 0 mg

18-Moroccan Carrot Soup

Time: 35 minutes

Serve: 4

Ingredients:

- 12 large carrots, peel and diced
- 2 tbsp coriander
- 1 tbsp ginger, grated
- 1 tsp turmeric
- 1 tsp cinnamon
- ½ cup water
- 14 oz coconut milk
- 1 tbsp honey
- 2 tsp garlic paste
- 1 red pepper, diced
- 1 large onion, diced
- Pepper
- Salt

Directions:

- Add all ingredients to the soup maker and stir well.
- Cover soup maker with lid and cook for 25 minutes on blend mode.
- Season with pepper and salt.
- Serve warm and enjoy.

Nutritional Value (Amount per Serving):

- Calories 368
- Fat 23.9 g
- Carbohydrates 39.1 g
- Sugar 21.4 g
- Protein 5.1 g
- Cholesterol 0 mg

19-Mixed Vegetable Soup

Time: 30 minutes

Serve: 4

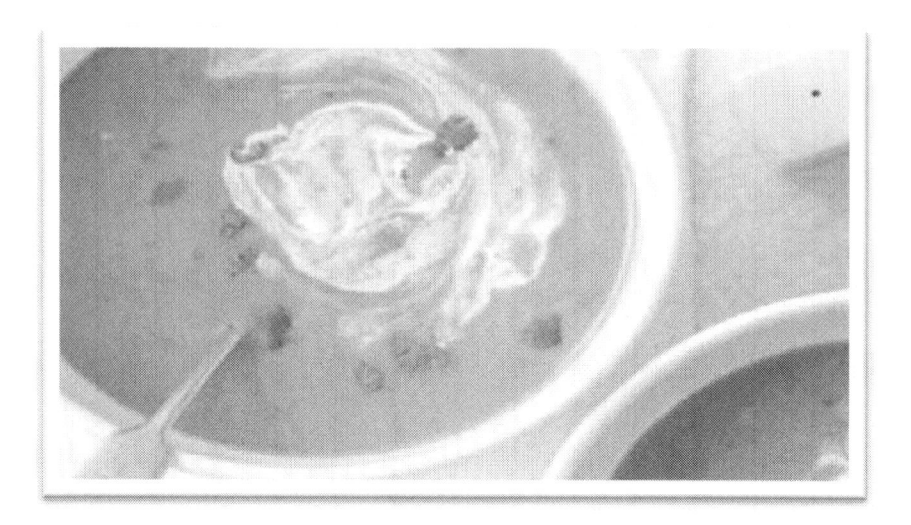

Ingredients:

- 3 cups mixed vegetables, chopped
- 1 tbsp curry powder
- 1 cup vegetable stock
- 1 ½ tbsp garlic, chopped
- 1 medium potato, chopped
- Pepper
- Salt

Directions:

- Add all ingredients to the soup maker.
- Add water to the soup maker up to the minimum mark.
- Cover soup maker with lid and cook on smooth mode.

- Season with pepper and salt.
- Serve and enjoy.

Nutritional Value (Amount per Serving):

- Calories 120
- Fat 1.3 g
- Carbohydrates 24.9 g
- Sugar 1 g
- Protein 4.1 g
- Cholesterol 0 mg

20-Delicious Sweet Corn Soup

Time: 40 minutes

Serve: 6

Ingredients:

- 2 medium corn cobs
- 6 ½ cups water
- 1 tsp butter
- 2 tsp corn flour
- 1 cup mixed vegetables
- 4 tbsp vegetable broth powder
- Pepper
- Salt

Directions:

- Add all ingredients to the soup maker except corn flour.
- Cover soup maker with lid and cook on blend mode.
- Meanwhile, in a small bowl, mix together corn flour and 3 tbsp water.
- Once 20 minutes is over then add cornflour slurry to the soup maker.
- Cover soup maker again and cook on the same mode for 10 minutes.
- Season with pepper and salt.
- Serve warm and enjoy.

Nutritional Value (Amount per Serving):

- Calories 109
- Fat 1.8 g
- Carbohydrates 20.9 g
- Sugar 1.7 g
- Protein 1.2 g
- Cholesterol 2 mg

21-Flavours Mediterranean Veggie Soup

Time: 35 minutes

Serve: 4

Ingredients:

- 2 tbsp cream cheese
- 2 tsp garlic paste
- 1 tsp thyme
- 1 tsp chives
- 1 tbsp oregano
- ¼ cup water
- 14 oz can tomatoes
- 1 small sweet potato, peeled and diced
- 1 large potato, peeled and diced
- 1 large leek, chopped
- 5 large carrots, peeled and diced

- 3.5 oz green beans, chopped
- 1 small red pepper, chopped
- 1 large onion, chopped
- Pepper
- Salt

Directions:

- Add all ingredients to the soup maker except cheese and stir well.
- If can tomatoes have not much water then add a little water and stir well.
- Cover soup maker with lid and cook for 25 minutes on basic mode.
- Stir in cheese and serve.

Nutritional Value (Amount per Serving):

- Calories 212
- Fat 2.2 g
- Carbohydrates 45.3 g
- Sugar 13.9 g
- Protein 5.9 g
- Cholesterol 6 mg

22-Easy Tomato Pepper Soup

Time: 35 minutes

Serve: 6

Ingredients:

- 1 garlic clove, chopped
- 1 vegetable stock cube
- 2 tbsp tomato paste
- 1 onion, chopped
- 3 peppers, chopped
- 8 tomatoes, chopped
- Pepper
- Salt

Directions:

- Add all ingredients to the soup maker.
- Pour water into the soup maker up to the 1.6-liter mark.
- Cover soup maker with lid and cook on smooth mode.
- Season with pepper and salt.
- Serve and enjoy.

Nutritional Value (Amount per Serving):

- Calories 44
- Fat 0.4 g
- Carbohydrates 9.5 g
- Sugar 5.8 g
- Protein 2 g
- Cholesterol 0 mg

23-Yummy Chicken Noodle Soup

Time: 25 minutes

Serve: 4

Ingredients:

- 4 cups chicken stock
- 1 lemon juice
- 3 garlic cloves, crushed
- 3.5 oz egg noodles
- 2 medium carrots, peeled and chopped
- 2 medium potatoes, peeled and cubed
- 8.8 oz chicken, cooked and shredded
- Pepper
- Salt

Directions:

- Break noodles into the small pieces.
- Add all ingredients to the soup maker.
- Cover soup maker with lid and cook on chunky mode for 15 minutes.
- Season with pepper and salt.
- Serve hot and enjoy.

Nutritional Value (Amount per Serving):

- Calories 230
- Fat 3.2 g
- Carbohydrates 27.7 g
- Sugar 3.8 g
- Protein 22.2 g
- Cholesterol 55 mg

24-Mix Herbed Potato Leek Soup

Time: 30 minutes

Serve: 4

Ingredients:

- ½ cup creme fraiche
- 1 tsp mixed herbs
- 1 vegetable stock cube
- 1 tbsp butter
- 4 medium potatoes, peeled and chopped
- 2 leeks, sliced
- 1 small onion, chopped
- Pepper
- Salt

Directions:

- Add all ingredients to the soup maker.
- Pour water into the soup maker up to the 1.6-liter mark or maximum fill line of soup maker.
- Cover soup maker with lid and cook on smooth mode.
- Season with pepper and salt.
- Serve warm and enjoy.

Nutritional Value (Amount per Serving):

- Calories 269
- Fat 9.3 g
- Carbohydrates 42.8 g
- Sugar 5 g
- Protein 5.4 g
- Cholesterol 20 mg

25-Spicy Chili Pepper Soup

Time: 30 minutes

Serve: 3

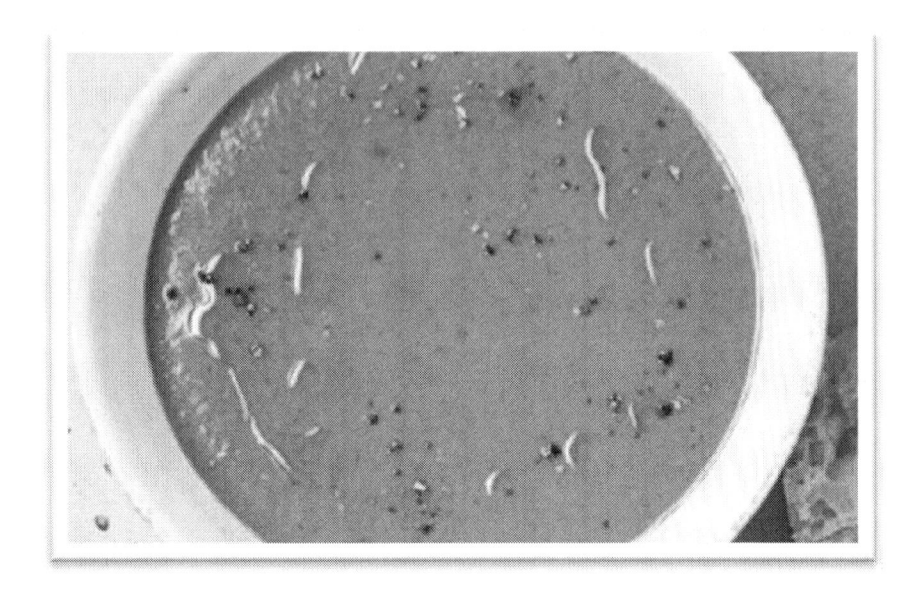

Ingredients:

- 3 cups chicken stock
- 1 medium potato, peeled and chopped
- 2 red chilies, sliced
- 2 garlic cloves, crushed
- 2 red peppers, chopped
- 1 onion, chopped
- 1 tbsp olive oil
- Pepper
- Salt

Directions:

- Heat olive oil in a pan over medium heat.
- Once the oil is hot then add garlic and onion and sauté until onion is softened.
- Add red chilies and sauté for 2 minutes.
- Transfer sautéed onion mixture to the soup maker.
- Add remaining ingredients to the soup maker.
- Cover soup maker with lid and cook on smooth mode.
- Season with pepper and salt.
- Serve and enjoy.

Nutritional Value (Amount per Serving):

- Calories 134
- Fat 5.5 g
- Carbohydrates 19.9 g
- Sugar 4.4 g
- Protein 3.2 g
- Cholesterol 0 mg

26-Root Vegetable Soup

Time: 30 minutes

Serve: 4

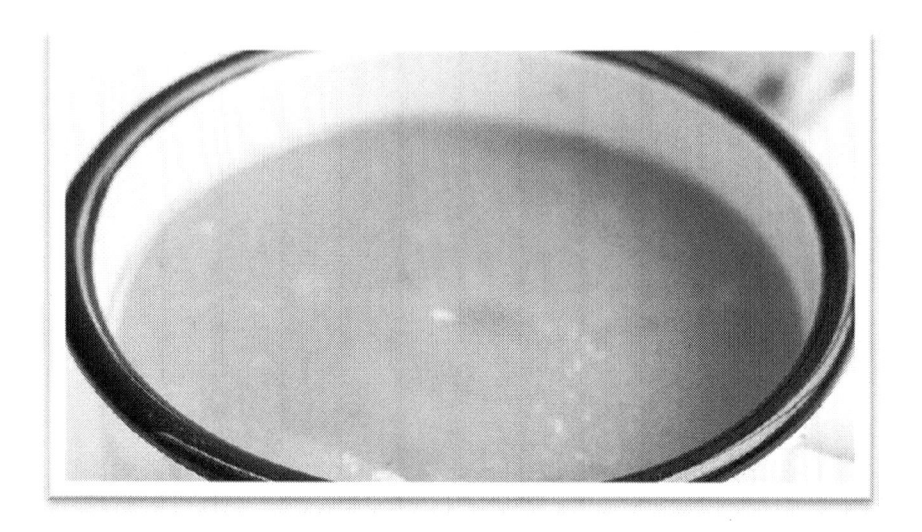

Ingredients:

- 2 carrots, peeled and chopped
- 1 fresh thyme sprigs
- 1 ½ cups vegetable stock
- 3 garlic cloves
- 1 red pepper, chopped
- 1 medium sweet potato, peeled and cubed
- 2 cups butternut squash, peeled and cubed
- 1 celery stalk, chopped
- 1 parsnip, peeled and cubed
- Pepper
- Salt

Directions:

- Add all ingredients to the soup maker.
- Cover soup maker with lid and cook on smooth mode.
- Season with pepper and salt.
- Serve warm and enjoy.

Nutritional Value (Amount per Serving):

- Calories 116
- Fat 1.1 g
- Carbohydrates 27.8 g
- Sugar 9.1 g
- Protein 2.5 g
- Cholesterol 0 mg

27-Spicy Potato Squash Soup

Time: 30 minutes

Serve: 4

Ingredients:

- ½ tsp red chili flakes
- 2 vegetable stock cubes
- 1/3 cup onion, chopped
- 2 ½ cups sweet potato, peeled and diced
- 2 ½ cups butternut squash, diced

Directions:

- Add all ingredients to the soup maker.
- Add boiling water to the soup maker up to 1.6-liter mark.
- Cover soup maker with lid and cook on smooth mode.
- Serve and enjoy.

Nutritional Value (Amount per Serving):

- Calories 161
- Fat 0.5 g
- Carbohydrates 37.6 g
- Sugar 10.5 g
- Protein 3.7 g
- Cholesterol 0 mg

28-Simple Swede Soup

Time: 30 minutes

Serve: 4

Ingredients:

- 1.1 lb. swede, chopped in cubes
- 2 vegetable stock cubes
- 1 tsp curry powder
- 2 carrots, sliced

Directions:

- Add all ingredients to the soup maker.
- Add boiling water to the soup maker up to 1.6-liter mark.
- Cover soup maker with lid and cook on smooth mode.
- Serve warm and enjoy.

Nutritional Value (Amount per Serving):

- Calories 64
- Fat 0.5 g
- Carbohydrates 14 g
- Sugar 8.5 g
- Protein 2 g
- Cholesterol 0 mg

29-Pea Mint Soup

Time: 30 minutes

Serve: 4

Ingredients:

- 1 tbsp parsley
- 1 tsp garlic paste
- 1 cup water
- 1 tbsp mozzarella cheese
- 1 tsp fresh mint
- 2 tbsp yogurt
- 2 onion, chopped
- 1 lb frozen peas
- Pepper
- Salt

Directions:

- Add all ingredients to the soup maker.
- Cover soup maker with lid and cook for 25 minutes on blend mode.
- Season with pepper and salt.
- Serve and enjoy.

Nutritional Value (Amount per Serving):

- Calories 138
- Fat 1.7 g
- Carbohydrates 22.5 g
- Sugar 8.2 g
- Protein 9 g
- Cholesterol 4 mg

30-Healthy Pea Soup

Time: 30 minutes

Serve: 4

Ingredients:

- 1 lb frozen peas
- 1 tbsp butter
- 2 ¾ cups vegetable stock
- ¼ cup parsley
- ¼ cup mint leaves
- 2 onions, chopped
- Pepper
- Salt

Directions:

- Add all ingredients to the soup maker.
- Cover soup maker with lid and cook on smooth mode.
- Season with pepper and salt.
- Serve warm and enjoy.

Nutritional Value (Amount per Serving):

- Calories 147
- Fat 4.7 g
- Carbohydrates 23.4 g
- Sugar 9 g
- Protein 6.8 g
- Cholesterol 8 mg

31-Pea Leek Soup

Time: 30 minutes

Serve: 4

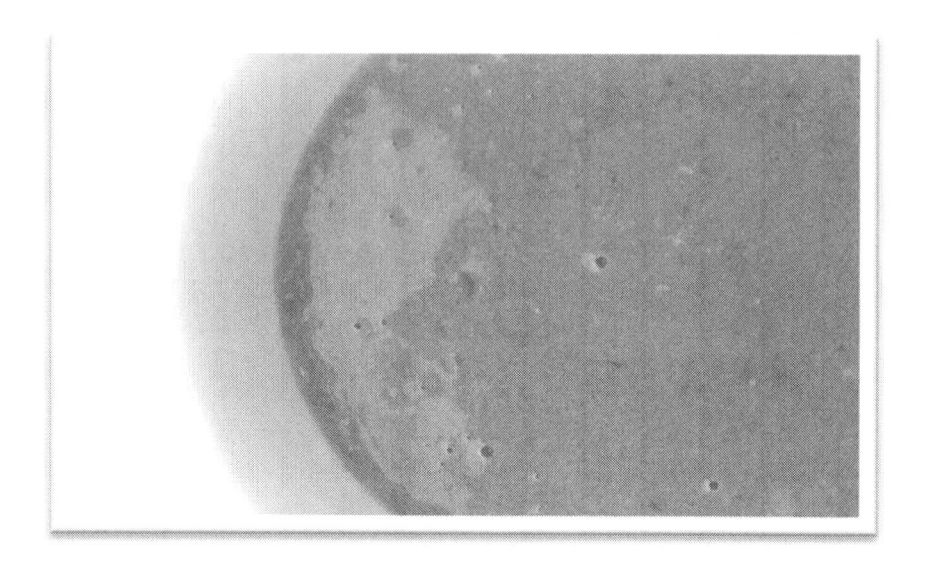

Ingredients:

- 2 tbsp mint leaves
- ½ cup white wine
- 4 cups vegetable stock
- 1 lb peas
- 1 leek, chopped
- 2 medium onion, chopped
- 1 tbsp butter
- Pepper
- Salt

Directions:

- Melt butter in a pan over medium heat.
- Once butter is melted then add onion and leek and sauté until onion is softened.
- Transfer onion mixture to the soup maker.
- Add remaining ingredients to the soup maker.
- Cover soup maker with lid and cook on smooth mode.
- Season with pepper and salt.
- Serve and enjoy.

Nutritional Value (Amount per Serving):

- Calories 189
- Fat 5.5 g
- Carbohydrates 27.7 g
- Sugar 11.9 g
- Protein 7.2 g
- Cholesterol 8 mg

32-Pea Ham Soup

Time: 30 minutes

Serve: 4

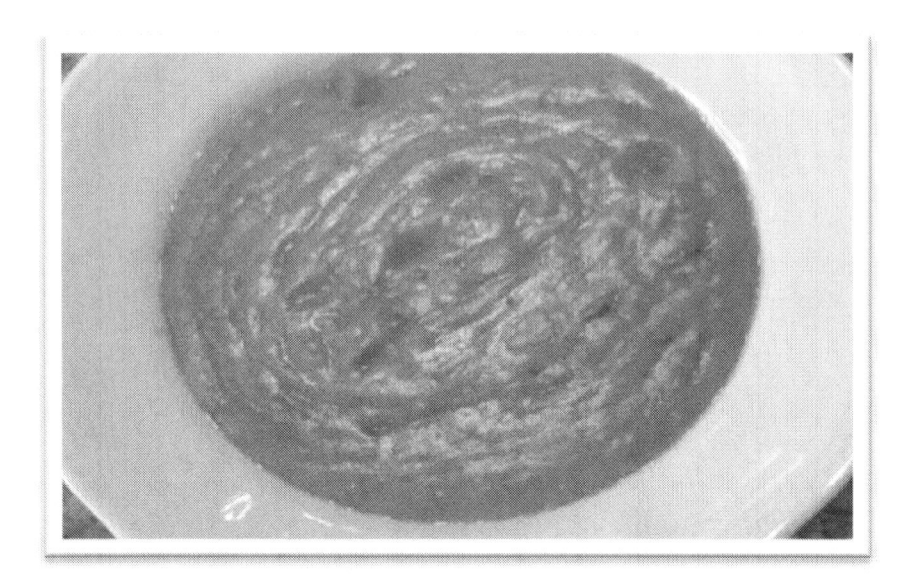

Ingredients:

- ½ cup ham, cooked and shredded
- ½ cup double cream
- 1 vegetable stock cube
- ½ cup baby spinach
- 1 lb frozen peas
- 6 spring onions, chopped
- Water
- Pepper
- Salt

Directions:

- Add all ingredients except cream to the soup maker.
- Add water to the soup maker up to the maximum mark.
- Cover soup maker with lid and cook on smooth mode.
- Season with pepper and salt.
- Serve and enjoy.

Nutritional Value (Amount per Serving):

- Calories 176
- Fat 7.4 g
- Carbohydrates 19.1 g
- Sugar 5.8 g
- Protein 9.5 g
- Cholesterol 30 mg

33-Healthy Green Soup

Time: 35 minutes

Serve: 4

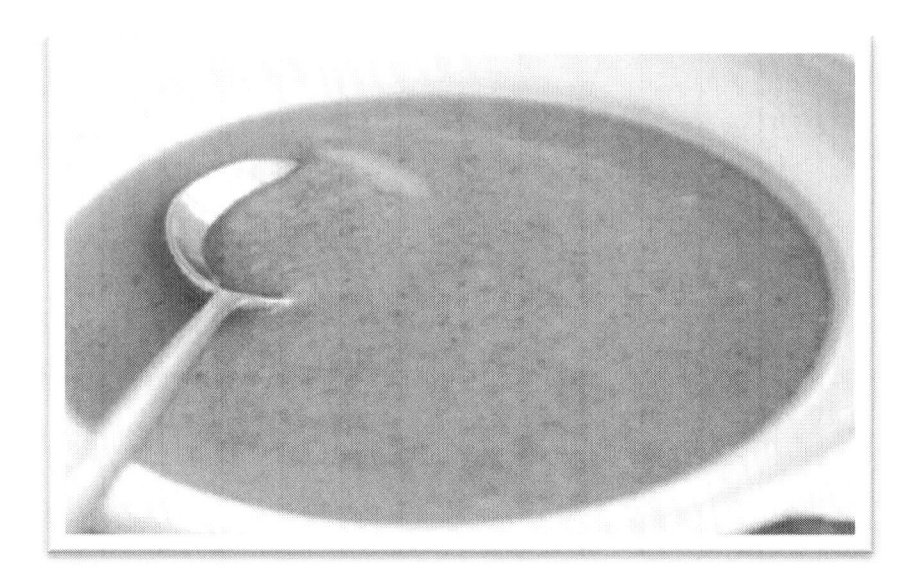

Ingredients:

- ½ cup water
- 1 tsp mustard
- 1 tsp parsley
- 1 tsp thyme
- 2 cups broccoli florets
- 1 green pepper, chopped
- 1 medium courgette, chopped
- 1/3 large cabbage, chopped
- Pepper
- Salt

Directions:

- Add all ingredients to the soup maker.
- Cover soup maker with lid and cook for 25 minutes on blend mode.
- Season with pepper and salt.
- Serve warm and enjoy.

Nutritional Value (Amount per Serving):

- Calories 60
- Fat 0.7 g
- Carbohydrates 12.6 g
- Sugar 5.7 g
- Protein 3.7 g
- Cholesterol 0 mg

34-Easy Pumpkin Soup

Time: 30 minutes

Serve: 4

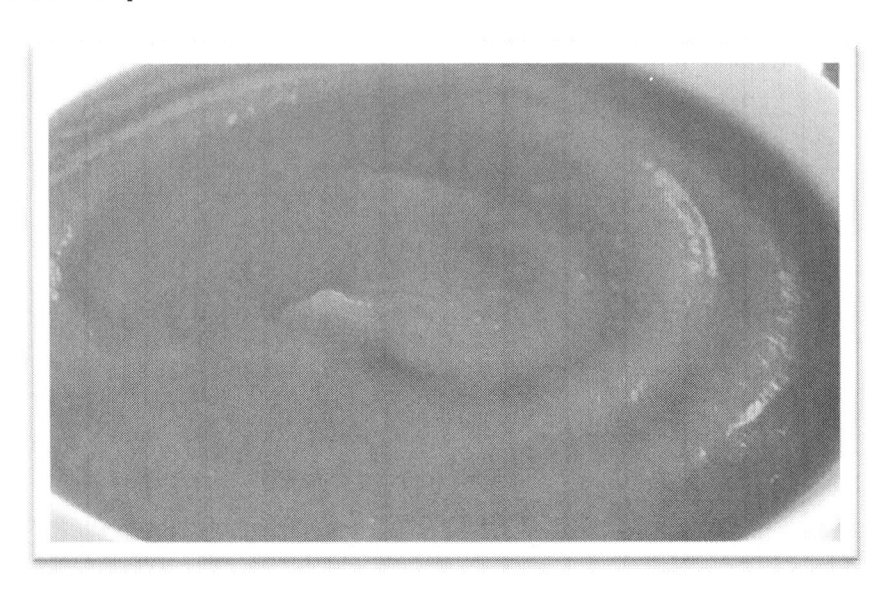

Ingredients:

- 1 cup cream
- 2 ¼ cup vegetable stock
- 1 medium potato, diced
- 4 cups pumpkin, diced
- 1 onion, diced
- 2 garlic cloves, minced
- Pepper
- Salt

Directions:

- Add all ingredients to the soup maker.
- Cover soup maker with lid and cook on smooth mode.
- Season with pepper and salt.
- Serve with bread and enjoy.

Nutritional Value (Amount per Serving):

- Calories 182
- Fat 5.2 g
- Carbohydrates 35.2 g
- Sugar 12 g
- Protein 4.7 g
- Cholesterol 11 mg

35-Cheddar Broccoli Soup

Time: 35 minutes

Serve: 6

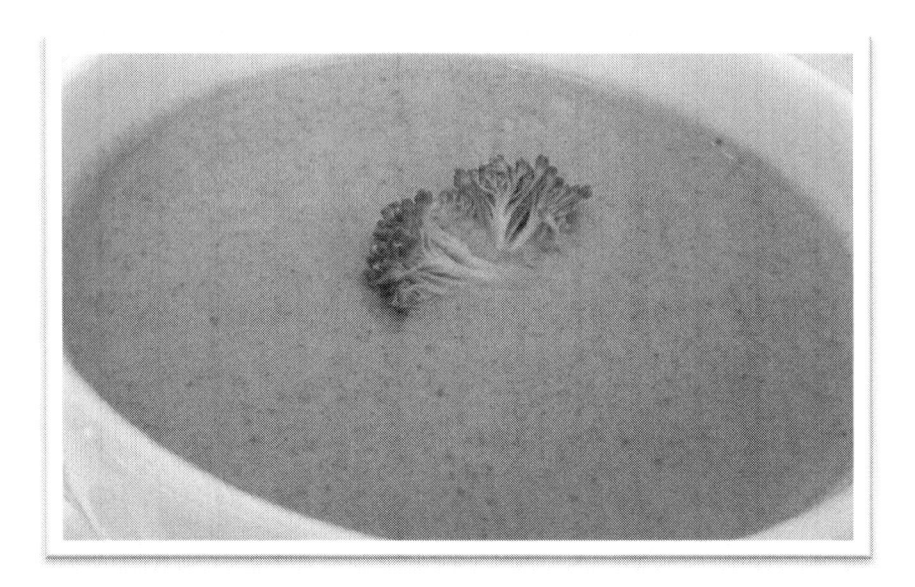

Ingredients:

- 1 tsp garlic paste
- 4 cups broccoli florets
- 1 cup cheddar cheese, grated
- ½ carrot, diced
- 1 large potato, diced
- 1 onion, diced
- 1 chicken stock cube
- 2 ½ cups water
- Pepper
- Salt

Directions:

- Add all ingredients to the soup maker.
- Cover soup maker with lid and cook for 25 minutes on blend mode.
- Season with pepper and salt.
- Serve warm and enjoy.

Nutritional Value (Amount per Serving):

- Calories 156
- Fat 6.6 g
- Carbohydrates 17.6 g
- Sugar 2.6 g
- Protein 8 g
- Cholesterol 20 mg

36-Flavorful Broccoli Soup

Time: 30 minutes

Serve: 4

Ingredients:

- 2 tbsp yogurt
- 2 cups of water
- 1 tsp thyme
- 1 tsp oregano
- 1 small onion, chopped
- 4 cups broccoli florets
- 1/5 medium courgette, chopped
- Pepper
- Salt

Directions:

- Add all ingredients except yogurt to the soup maker.
- Cover soup maker with lid and cook for 25 minutes on blend mode.
- Add yogurt and stir well. Season with pepper and salt.
- Serve and enjoy.

Nutritional Value (Amount per Serving):

- Calories 47
- Fat 0.5 g
- Carbohydrates 9 g
- Sugar 3 g
- Protein 3.4 g
- Cholesterol 0 mg

37-Simple Carrot Broccoli Soup

Time: 30 minutes

Serve: 4

Ingredients:

- 2 cups broccoli florets
- 2 cups carrot, diced
- 1 cup cauliflower florets
- 1 vegetable stock cube
- Water
- Pepper
- Salt

Directions:

- Add all ingredients to the soup maker.
- Pour water into the soup maker up to the 1.3-liter mark.
- Cover soup maker with lid and cook on smooth mode.

- Season with pepper and salt.
- Serve and enjoy.

Nutritional Value (Amount per Serving):

- Calories 44
- Fat 0.2g
- Carbohydrates 9.8 g
- Sugar 4.1 g
- Protein 2.2 g
- Cholesterol 0 mg

38-Simple Cauliflower Broccoli Soup

Time: 30 minutes

Serve: 4

Ingredients:

- ½ medium onion, chopped
- 1 tbsp olive oil
- 4 cups water
- 2 vegetable stock cubes
- 2 cups broccoli, chopped
- ½ head cauliflower, cut into florets
- Pepper
- Salt

Directions:

- Heat olive oil in a pan over medium heat.
- Once the oil is hot then add onion and sauté until softened.
- Transfer sautéed onion to the soup maker.
- Add remaining ingredients to the soup maker.
- Cover soup maker with lid and cook on smooth mode.
- Season with pepper and salt.
- Serve warm and enjoy.

Nutritional Value (Amount per Serving):

- Calories 64
- Fat 3.9 g
- Carbohydrates 6.7 g
- Sugar 2.2 g
- Protein 2.3 g
- Cholesterol 0 mg

39-Winter Vegetable Soup

Time: 40 minutes

Serve: 4

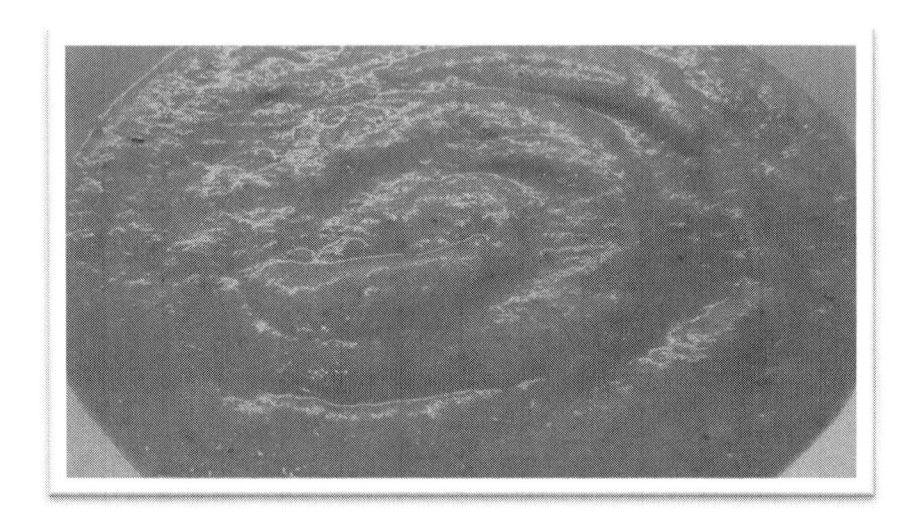

Ingredients:

- 1 tsp ground cumin
- 2 ¾ cups vegetable stock
- 1 small sweet potato, peeled and diced
- 2 parsnips, diced
- 4 celery stalk, chopped
- 1 onion, chopped
- 3 carrots, peeled and chopped
- 1 leek, chopped
- Pepper
- Salt

Directions:

- Add all ingredients except cumin to the soup maker.
- Cover soup maker with lid and cook on chunky mode.
- Once 28 minutes are over then select blend mode to the desired consistency.
- Stir in ground cumin, pepper, and salt.
- Serve and enjoy.

Nutritional Value (Amount per Serving):

- Calories 125
- Fat 1.9 g
- Carbohydrates 29.1 g
- Sugar 10.7 g
- Protein 2.6 g
- Cholesterol 0 mg

40-Black Bean Potato Soup

Time: 40 minutes

Serve: 4

Ingredients:

- 3 ½ cups vegetable stock
- 1 tsp ground cumin
- 1 tsp cayenne pepper
- 1 small onion, chopped
- 1.5 cans black beans
- 2 garlic cloves, chopped
- 2 celery stalks, chopped
- 1 red pepper, sliced
- 2 small sweet potatoes, peeled and chopped
- 2 medium carrots, sliced
- Pepper
- Salt

Directions:

- Add all ingredients to the soup maker.
- Cover soup maker with lid and cook on chunky mode.
- Once 28 minutes are over then set soup maker to the blend mode until your desired soup consistency.
- Season with pepper and salt.
- Serve and enjoy.

Nutritional Value (Amount per Serving):

- Calories 364
- Fat 4.3 g
- Carbohydrates 70.7 g
- Sugar 8.2 g
- Protein 16.9 g
- Cholesterol 0 mg

41-Apple Carrot Soup

Time: 30 minutes

Serve: 6

Ingredients:

- 1 lb carrots, peeled and chopped
- 3 ½ cups vegetable stock
- ½ tsp cinnamon
- 1 tsp nutmeg
- 1 tsp olive oil
- 1 garlic clove, crushed
- 2 medium apple, peeled, cored and diced
- 1 onion, diced
- Pepper
- Salt

Directions:

- Heat olive oil in a pan over medium heat.
- Add garlic and onion and sauté until onion is softened.
- Add nutmeg and stir well. Transfer sautéed onion mixture to the soup maker.
- Add remaining ingredients to the soup maker.
- Cover soup maker with lid and cook on smooth mode.
- Season with pepper and salt.
- Serve and enjoy.

Nutritional Value (Amount per Serving):

- Calories 93
- Fat 2.2 g
- Carbohydrates 21.1 g
- Sugar 13.5 g
- Protein 1.1 g
- Cholesterol 0 mg

42-Sweet Squash Apple Soup

Time: 30 minutes

Serve: 4

Ingredients:

- 1 cup water
- 2 tbsp yogurt
- 2 tsp garlic paste
- 1 tsp ginger paste
- 1 tsp paprika
- 1 tsp mixed spice
- 2 tsp coriander powder
- 1 tsp cumin
- ½ cup pumpkin
- 2 cups butternut squash
- 1 onion, chopped

- 3 medium apples, peeled, cored, and diced
- Pepper
- Salt

Directions:

- Add all ingredients except yogurt to the soup maker.
- Cover soup maker with lid and cook for 25 minutes on blend mode.
- Add yogurt and stir well. Season with pepper and salt.
- Serve warm and enjoy.

Nutritional Value (Amount per Serving):

- Calories 153
- Fat 0.8 g
- Carbohydrates 38.2 g
- Sugar 21.8 g
- Protein 2.5 g
- Cholesterol 0 mg

43-Creamy Parsnip Apple Soup

Time: 30 minutes

Serve: 6

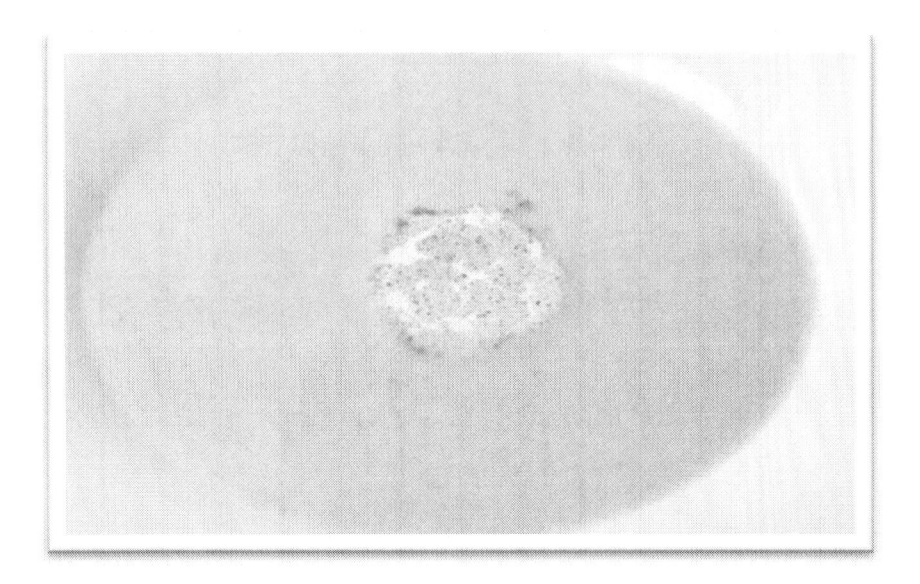

Ingredients:

- 1 tbsp butter
- 5 oz milk
- 4 cups vegetable stock
- 1 lb apples, peeled, cored, and chopped
- 2 garlic cloves, crushed
- 1 lb parsnips, cut into pieces
- 2 medium onions, chopped
- 1 tbsp olive oil
- Pepper
- Salt

Directions:

- Heat butter and olive oil in a pan over medium heat.
- Add parsnips and onion to the pan and sauté until onion is softened.
- Add garlic and apples and sauté for 2 minutes.
- Transfer sautéed onion mixture to the soup maker.
- Add remaining ingredients to the soup maker.
- Cover soup maker with lid and cook on smooth mode.
- Season with pepper and salt.
- Serve warm and enjoy.

Nutritional Value (Amount per Serving):

- Calories 143
- Fat 5.4 g
- Carbohydrates 24 g
- Sugar 10.5 g
- Protein 2.3 g
- Cholesterol 7 mg

44-Apple Cauliflower Soup

Time: 35 minutes

Serve: 4

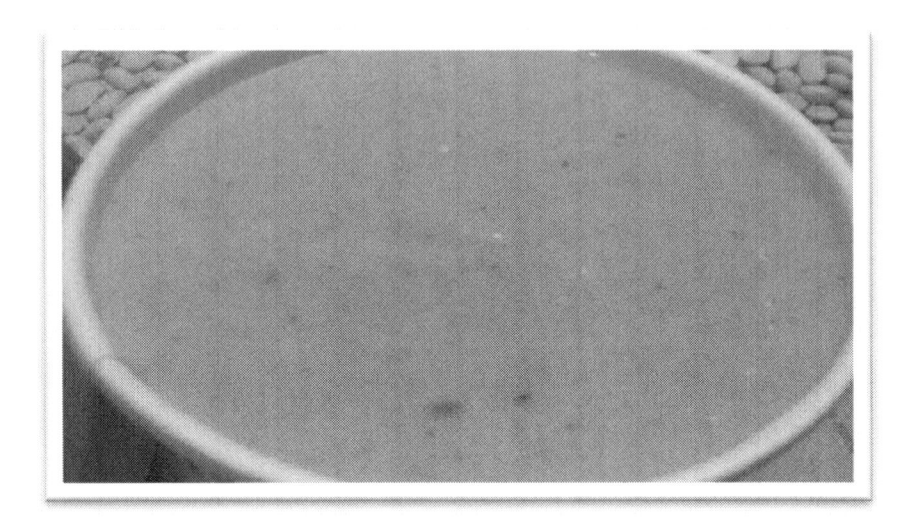

Ingredients:

- 2 tsp curry powder
- 3 cups vegetable stock
- 2 medium apples, peeled and sliced
- 1 small cauliflower head, chopped
- 2 garlic cloves, sliced
- 1 onion, chopped
- 2 tbsp olive oil

Directions:

- Heat oil in a pan over medium heat.
- Add onion and garlic and sauté until onion is softened.
- Add cauliflower to the pan and sauté for 2 minutes.

- Transfer sautéed onion mixture to the soup maker.
- Add remaining ingredients to the soup maker.
- Cover soup maker with lid and cook for 25 minutes on blend mode.
- Serve and enjoy.

Nutritional Value (Amount per Serving):

- Calories 159
- Fat 9 g
- Carbohydrates 24.1 g
- Sugar 15.9 g
- Protein 2.1 g
- Cholesterol 0 mg

45-Simple Apple Parsnip Soup

Time: 30 minutes

Serve: 4

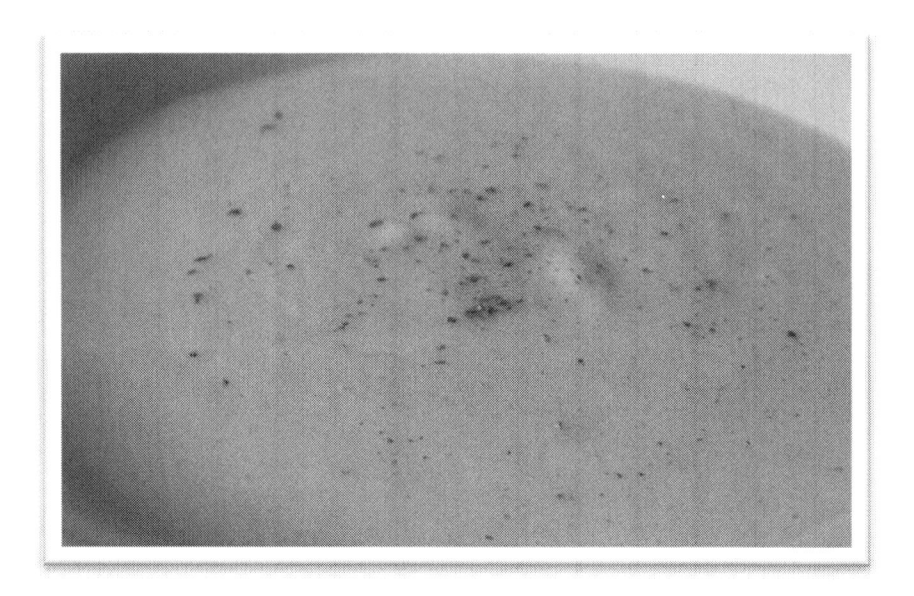

Ingredients:

- 2 cups parsnips, chopped
- 2 apples, peeled, cored, and chopped
- 2 garlic cloves, crushed
- 2 medium onion, chopped
- 4 cups vegetable stock
- Pepper
- Salt

Directions:

- Add all ingredients to the soup maker.
- Cover soup maker with lid and cook on smooth mode.

- Season with pepper and salt.
- Serve and enjoy.

Nutritional Value (Amount per Serving):

- Calories 142
- Fat 2.5 g
- Carbohydrates 35 g
- Sugar 19.1 g
- Protein 1.8 g
- Cholesterol 0 mg

46-Tasty Red Lentil Soup

Time: 30 minutes

Serve: 4

Ingredients:

- 1 cup split red lentils, rinsed and soak in water for 30 minutes
- 1 onion, chopped
- 4 cups vegetable stock
- 1 large potato, peeled and diced
- Pepper
- Salt

Directions:

- Add all ingredients to the soup maker.
- Cover soup maker with lid and cook on smooth mode.
- Season with pepper and salt.
- Serve warm with bread.

Nutritional Value (Amount per Serving):

- Calories 254
- Fat 1.1 g
- Carbohydrates 48.1 g
- Sugar 3.4 g
- Protein 14.5 g
- Cholesterol 0 mg

47-Lentil Vegetable Soup

Time: 30 minutes

Serve: 4

Ingredients:

- 3 ½ cups vegetable stock
- 1 vegetable stock cube
- 1 tsp ground cinnamon
- 1 garlic clove, minced
- ¼ cup lentils, rinsed and soaked in water for 30 minutes
- 1 lb mixed vegetables
- Pepper
- Salt

Directions:

- Add all ingredients to the soup maker.
- Cover soup maker with lid and cook on smooth mode.
- Season with pepper and salt.
- Serve and enjoy.

Nutritional Value (Amount per Serving):

- Calories 95
- Fat 2.2 g
- Carbohydrates 17.8 g
- Sugar 2 g
- Protein 4.8 g
- Cholesterol 0 mg

48-Red Lentil Sweet Potato Soup

Time: 30 minutes

Serve: 4

Ingredients:

- 1 tbsp tomato paste
- ½ tsp chili powder
- 2 vegetable stock cubes
- 1 tsp ground ginger
- ¼ tsp ground cumin
- 1 cup red lentils, rinsed and soaked in water for 30 minutes
- 2 sweet potatoes, peeled and diced
- 1 garlic cloves, minced
- 1 onion, diced
- 4 cups water
- Pepper
- Salt

Directions:

- Add all ingredients to the soup maker.
- Cover soup maker with lid and cook on smooth mode.
- Season with pepper and salt.
- Serve and enjoy.

Nutritional Value (Amount per Serving):

- Calories 249
- Fat 0.9 g
- Carbohydrates 46.7 g
- Sugar 5.4 g
- Protein 14.2 g
- Cholesterol 0 mg

49-Chunky Squash Soup

Time: 40 minutes

Serve: 4

Ingredients:

- 4 cups water
- 2 tbsp oats
- 2 vegetable stock cubes
- 1 bay leaf
- 1 tsp thyme
- 1 tsp ground ginger
- 1 tsp ground coriander
- 2 garlic cloves, minced
- 1 onion, chopped
- 1 large butternut squash, peeled, deseeded, and diced
- Pepper
- Salt

Directions:

- Add all ingredients to the soup maker.
- Cover soup maker with lid and cook on chunky mode.
- Season with pepper and salt.
- Serve hot and enjoy.

Nutritional Value (Amount per Serving):

- Calories 73
- Fat 0.6 g
- Carbohydrates 17.1 g
- Sugar 1.2 g
- Protein 1.9 g
- Cholesterol 0 mg

50-Delicious Cauliflower Curried Soup

Time:35 minutes

Serve: 4

Ingredients:

- 2 vegetable stock cubes
- 4 ½ cups water
- 1 tsp garam masala
- 1 tsp ground coriander
- ½ tsp ground cumin
- 1 tsp turmeric
- 1 sweet potato, peeled and diced
- 1 large cauliflower head, chopped
- 1 tbsp ginger, grated
- 2 garlic cloves, minced
- 1 onion, diced
- 1 tbsp olive oil
- Pepper
- Salt

Directions:

- Heat olive oil in a pan over medium heat.
- Add garlic and onion to the pan and sauté until softened.
- Add spices and sweet potato and sauté for 2 minutes.
- Transfer sautéed onion mixture to the soup maker.
- Add remaining ingredients to the soup maker.
- Cover soup maker with lid and cook on smooth mode.
- Season with pepper and salt.
- Serve and enjoy.

Nutritional Value (Amount per Serving):

- Calories 134
- Fat 4.2 g
- Carbohydrates 22.2 g
- Sugar 8.2 g
- Protein 5.6 g
- Cholesterol 0 mg

51-Yummy Chicken Chorizo Soup

Time: 45 minutes

Serve: 4

Ingredients:

- 3 cups water
- 1 can sweet corn, drained
- 1 can tomatoes, chopped
- 1 sweet potato, peeled and diced
- ¼ cup chorizo, diced
- 1 garlic clove, minced
- 1 large onion, diced
- 1 chicken breast, diced
- 1 tbsp olive oil
- Pepper
- Salt

Directions:

- Heat oil in a pan over medium heat.
- Add chicken to the pan and cook until chicken turns to golden brown.
- Add chorizo, garlic, and onions and sauté until softened.
- Transfer pan mixture to the soup maker.
- Add remaining ingredients to the soup maker.
- Cover soup maker with lid and cook on chunky mode.
- Serve warm and enjoy.

Nutritional Value (Amount per Serving):

- Calories 230
- Fat 10.2 g
- Carbohydrates 24.3 g
- Sugar 8.3 g
- Protein 12.6 g
- Cholesterol 30 mg

52-Onion Cheese Soup

Time: 45 minutes

Serve: 4

Ingredients:

- 1 cup cheddar cheese, grated
- 2 vegetable stock cubed
- 3 ½ cups water
- 1 tsp thyme
- 4 cups spring onions, head trimmed and chopped
- 2 medium potato, peeled and diced
- 1 garlic clove, chopped
- 1 tbsp olive oil
- Pepper
- Salt

Directions:

- Heat olive oil in a pan over medium heat.
- Add garlic, onion, and potato to the pan and sauté over low heat for 10 minutes.
- Transfer pan mixture to the soup maker along with remaining ingredients except for cheese.
- Cover soup maker with lid and cook for 25 minutes on blend mode.
- Add grated cheese and stir well.
- Serve hot and enjoy.

Nutritional Value (Amount per Serving):

- Calories 260
- Fat 13.2 g
- Carbohydrates 26.7 g
- Sugar 3.3 g
- Protein 11.1 g
- Cholesterol 30 mg

53-Roasted Pepper Soup

Time: 1 hour

Serve: 4

Ingredients:

- 1 tsp ground turmeric
- 2 vegetable stock cubes
- 3 ½ cups water
- 2 medium onion, sliced
- 2 celery stalks, chopped
- 3 red pepper, deseeded and sliced in half
- 2 garlic clove
- 2 cups broccoli florets
- Pepper
- Salt

Directions:

- Preheat the oven to 180 C.
- Place all vegetables on a baking dish and spray with cooking spray.
- Place in preheated oven and roast for 30 minutes.
- Transfer roasted vegetable to the soup maker.
- Add remaining ingredients to the soup maker.
- Cover soup maker with lid and cook on smooth mode.
- Serve and enjoy.

Nutritional Value (Amount per Serving):

- Calories 77
- Fat 0.7 g
- Carbohydrates 16.6 g
- Sugar 7.8 g
- Protein 3.2 g
- Cholesterol 0 mg

54-Chickpea Cabbage Soup

Time: 45 minutes

Serve: 4

Ingredients:

- 2 vegetable stock cubes
- 14 oz can chickpeas, drained
- 1 ¼ cups cabbage, shredded
- 14 oz can tomatoes, chopped
- 2 ¼ cups water
- 1 potato, peeled and diced
- 1 green chili, chopped
- 2 garlic cloves, minced
- 1 tbsp ginger, grated
- 1 onion, diced
- 1/2 tsp turmeric

- 1/2 tsp coriander powder
- 1/2 tsp cumin powder
- 1 tbsp olive oil
- Pepper
- Salt

Directions:

- Heat olive oil in a pan over medium heat.
- Add ginger, chili, garlic, and onion and sauté until onion is softened.
- Transfer sautéed onion mixture to the soup maker.
- Add remaining ingredients to the soup maker.
- Cover soup maker with lid and cook on chunky mode.
- Serve warm and enjoy.

Nutritional Value (Amount per Serving):

- Calories 232
- Fat 5.1 g
- Carbohydrates 41.1 g
- Sugar 5.7 g
- Protein 7.7 g
- Cholesterol 0 mg

55-Healthy Kale Soup

Time: 30 minutes

Serve: 4

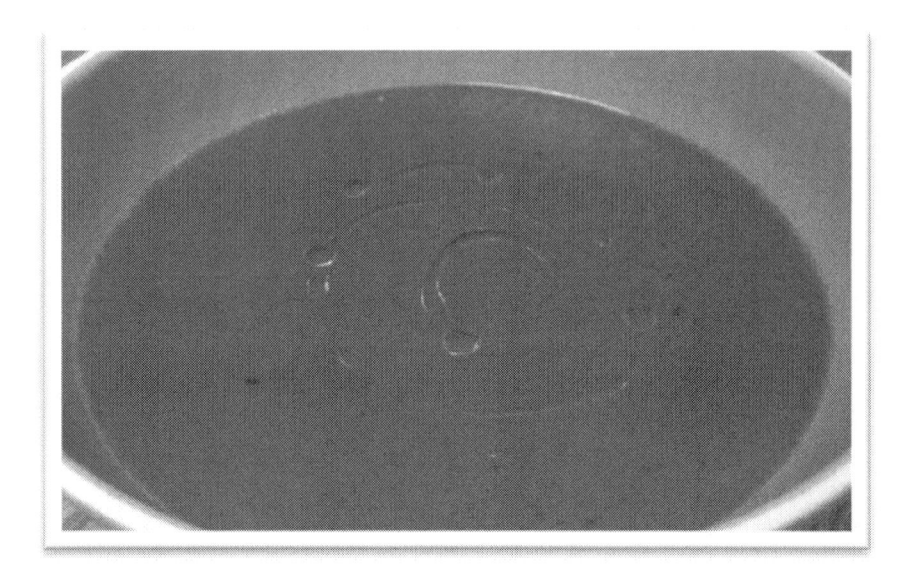

Ingredients:

- 3.5 oz kale
- 1 garlic clove, chopped
- 2 large tomatoes, chopped
- ¼ cup spring onions, sliced
- 1 celery stalk, chopped
- 1 large carrot, peeled and diced
- 1 potato, peeled and diced
- 2 vegetable stock cubes
- Water
- Pepper
- Salt

Directions:

- Add all ingredients to the soup maker.
- Pour water into the soup maker up to the 1.6-liter mark.
- Cover soup maker with lid and cook on smooth mode.
- Season with pepper and salt.
- Serve and enjoy.

Nutritional Value (Amount per Serving):

- Calories 77
- Fat 0.4 g
- Carbohydrates 16.8 g
- Sugar 3.8 g
- Protein 2.9 g
- Cholesterol 0 mg

56-Lentil Tomato Soup

Time: 30 minutes

Serve: 6

Ingredients:

- 1 tsp mixed herbs
- 1 vegetable stock cube
- 2 tbsp tomato paste
- 1 ¼ cups red lentils, rinsed and soaked in water for 30 minutes
- 1 large carrot, chopped
- 1 garlic clove, sliced
- 1 large onion, diced
- 14 oz can tomatoes, chopped
- Pepper
- Salt

Directions:

- Add all ingredients to the soup maker.
- Pour water in the soup maker up to 1.6-liter mark.
- Cover soup maker with lid and cook on smooth mode.
- Season with pepper and salt.
- Serve warm and enjoy.

Nutritional Value (Amount per Serving):

- Calories 176
- Fat 0.5 g
- Carbohydrates 32.2 g
- Sugar 5.4 g
- Protein 11.6 g
- Cholesterol 0 mg

57-Vegan Lentil Soup

Time: 30 minutes

Serve: 4

Ingredients:

- 2 tsp oregano
- 1 cup water
- 1 tsp chili powder
- 1 tsp ginger paste
- 1 tsp garlic paste
- 1 onion, chopped
- 1 large carrot, chopped
- 14 oz can tomatoes
- 1 cup yellow lentils, rinsed and soaked in water for 1 hour
- Pepper
- Salt

Directions:

- Add all ingredients to the soup maker.
- Cover soup maker with lid and cook on smooth mode.
- Season with pepper and salt.
- Serve with bread.

Nutritional Value (Amount per Serving):

- Calories 199
- Fat 0.7 g
- Carbohydrates 35.8 g
- Sugar 5.5 g
- Protein 13.6 g
- Cholesterol 0 mg

58-Spicy Lentil Carrot Soup

Time: 35 minutes

Serve: 4

Ingredients:

- 3 cups vegetable stock
- ¼ cup dried red lentils, rinsed and soaked in water for 30 minutes
- 2 large carrots, sliced
- 1 tsp garam masala
- 1 onion, chopped
- 1 tsp chili powder
- 2 garlic cloves, crushed
- 1 tbsp olive oil
- Pepper
- Salt

Directions:

- Heat oil in a pan over medium heat.
- Add garlic and onion and sauté until onion is softened.
- Add garam masala and sauté for a minute.
- Transfer pan mixture to the soup maker.
- Add remaining ingredients to the soup maker.
- Cover soup maker with lid and cook on smooth mode.
- Season with pepper and salt.
- Serve and enjoy.

Nutritional Value (Amount per Serving):

- Calories 110
- Fat 5.3 g
- Carbohydrates 15.7 g
- Sugar 4.8 g
- Protein 3.9 g
- Cholesterol 0 mg

59-Beetroot Soup

Time: 30 minutes

Serve: 4

Ingredients:

- 1 cup sour cream
- 2 ¾ cup vegetable stock
- 1 medium onion, chopped
- 1 lb beetroot, peel and chopped
- Pepper
- Salt

Directions:

- Add all ingredients except sour cream to the soup maker.
- Cover soup maker with lid and cook on smooth mode.

- Add sour cream and stir well.
- Season with pepper and salt.
- Serve warm and enjoy.

Nutritional Value (Amount per Serving):

- Calories 191
- Fat 13.7 g
- Carbohydrates 17.7 g
- Sugar 11.7 g
- Protein 4 g
- Cholesterol 25 mg

60-Orange Carrot Beetroot Soup

Time: 30 minutes

Serve: 4

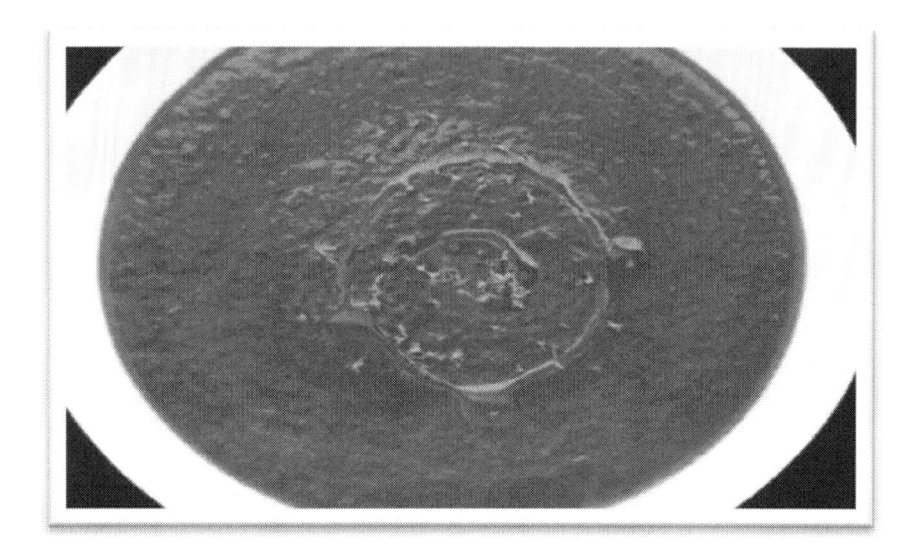

Ingredients:

- 3 ¼ cups hot water
- 1 vegetable stock cube
- 1 large carrot, chopped
- 1 large onion, chopped
- 1.3 lb beetroot, cooked and quartered
- 1 ½ cups orange juice
- Pepper
- Salt

Directions:

- Add all ingredients to the soup maker.
- Cover soup maker with lid and cook on smooth mode.
- Season with pepper and salt.
- Serve and enjoy.

Nutritional Value (Amount per Serving):

- Calories 129
- Fat 0.5 g
- Carbohydrates 29.6 g
- Sugar 22 g
- Protein 3.7 g
- Cholesterol 0 mg

61-Prawn Soup

Time: 30 minutes

Serve: 4

Ingredients:

- 1 cup cream
- 2 cups fish stock
- ¼ cup parsley, chopped
- 1/8 tsp cayenne pepper
- 1 tbsp tomato paste
- 1 small onion, chopped
- 1 garlic clove, chopped
- ¼ cup spring onion, chopped
- 1 tomato, chopped
- ½ lb prawns, peeled and deveined

Directions:

- Add all ingredients to the soup maker.
- Cover soup maker with lid and cook on smooth mode.
- Serve and enjoy.

Nutritional Value (Amount per Serving):

- Calories 143
- Fat 5.4 g
- Carbohydrates 6.7 g
- Sugar 3 g
- Protein 16.8 g
- Cholesterol 132 mg

62-Tofu Prawn Soup

Time: 45 minutes

Serve: 4

Ingredients:

- 7 oz tofu, diced
- 1 courgette, grated
- 1 sweet potato, peeled and grated
- 1 tbsp chili powder
- 1 chicken stock cube
- 4 ½ cups water
- 2 garlic cloves, minced
- 1 onion, sliced
- 4.5 oz prawns
- 1 tbsp olive oil
- Pepper
- Salt

Directions:

- Heat oil in a pan over medium heat.
- Add prawns in the pan and sauté until cooked. Remove pan from heat and set aside.
- Add remaining ingredients to the soup maker.
- Cover soup maker with lid and cook on chunky mode.
- Add cooked prawns to the soup and stir well.
- Season with pepper and salt.
- Serve warm and enjoy.

Nutritional Value (Amount per Serving):

- Calories 158
- Fat 6.7 g
- Carbohydrates 13.3 g
- Sugar 4.3 g
- Protein 13.3 g
- Cholesterol 67 mg

63-Delicious Fish Soup

Time: 30 minutes

Serve: 4

Ingredients:

- 1 large onion, chopped
- ¾ lbs haddock, cooked
- 2 cups fish stock
- 2 large potatoes, diced
- 1 tbsp olive oil
- Pepper
- Salt

Directions:

- Heat olive oil in a pan over medium heat.
- Add onion to the pan and sauté until softened.
- Transfer sautéed onion to the soup maker.
- Add remaining ingredients to the soup maker.
- Cover soup maker with lid and cook on smooth mode.
- Season with pepper and salt.
- Serve and enjoy.

Nutritional Value (Amount per Serving):

- Calories 287
- Fat 5.5 g
- Carbohydrates 32.5 g
- Sugar 3.7 g
- Protein 26.8 g
- Cholesterol 64 mg

64-Salmon Soup

Time: 30 minutes

Serve: 4

Ingredients:

- 1 tbsp olive oil
- 1 cup light cream
- 1 chicken stock cube
- 1 large potato, peeled and chopped
- ¾ lb smoked salmon
- Water

Directions:

- Add all ingredients to the soup maker.
- Pour water into the soup maker up to the minimum mark.
- Cover soup maker with lid and cook on smooth mode.
- Serve warm and enjoy.

Nutritional Value (Amount per Serving):

- Calories 291
- Fat 16.6 g
- Carbohydrates 17.3 g
- Sugar 0.8 g
- Protein 18.2 g
- Cholesterol 53 mg

65-Beef Soup

Time: 35 minutes

Serve: 4

Ingredients:

- 3 cups beef stock
- 14 oz can tomatoes, chopped
- 2 tsp mixed herbs
- 3 garlic cloves, minced
- 1 onion, chopped
- ½ lb ground beef, cooked
- 1 tbsp olive oil
- Pepper
- Salt

Directions:

- Heat oil in a pan over medium heat.
- Add onion to the pan and sauté until softened.
- Transfer sautéed onion to the soup maker.
- Add remaining ingredients to the soup maker.
- Cover soup maker with lid and cook on smooth mode.
- Season with pepper and salt.
- Serve and enjoy.

Nutritional Value (Amount per Serving):

- Calories 184
- Fat 7.5 g
- Carbohydrates 8.7 g
- Sugar 4.6 g
- Protein 20.6 g
- Cholesterol 51 mg

66-Tasty Mexican Soup

Time: 30 minutes

Serve: 4

Ingredients:

- 4 cups chicken stock
- 2 fresh lime juice
- 1 red chili, sliced
- 14 oz can tomatoes
- 1 tsp ground cumin
- 5 garlic cloves

Directions:

- Add all ingredients to the soup maker.
- Cover soup maker with lid and cook on smooth mode.
- Season with pepper and salt.
- Serve warm and enjoy.

Nutritional Value (Amount per Serving):

- Calories 44
- Fat 0.7 g
- Carbohydrates 9.1 g
- Sugar 4.5 g
- Protein 2 g
- Cholesterol 0 mg

67-Spicy Kidney Bean Soup

Time: 35 minutes

Serve: 4

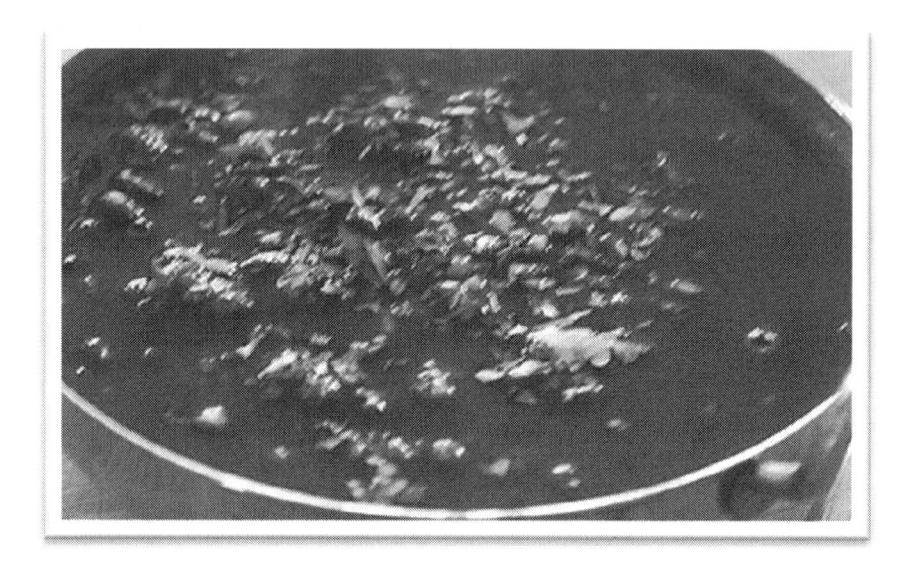

Ingredients:

- 1 lb red kidney beans
- 4 cups passata
- ½ tsp ground coriander
- ½ tsp ground cumin
- ½ tsp chili powder
- 2 garlic cloves, minced
- 1 onion, chopped
- 1 tbsp olive oil
- Pepper
- Salt

Directions:

- Heat oil in a pan over medium heat.
- Add garlic and onion and sauté until onion is softened.
- Add spices and sauté for a minute.
- Transfer sautéed onion mixture to the soup maker.
- Add remaining ingredients to the soup maker and stir well.
- Pour hot water into the soup maker up to the maximum mark.
- Cover soup maker with lid and cook on smooth mode.
- Season with pepper and salt.
- Serve warm and enjoy.

Nutritional Value (Amount per Serving):

- Calories 455
- Fat 5.1 g
- Carbohydrates 77.4 g
- Sugar 3.7 g
- Protein 27.3 g
- Cholesterol 0 mg

68-Easy Chili Sweet Potato Soup

Time: 35 minutes

Serve: 4

Ingredients:

- 3 ½ cups vegetable stock
- 2 red chilies, sliced
- 3 garlic cloves, minced
- 1 onion, peeled and chopped
- 2 lbs sweet potatoes, peeled and chopped
- 1 tbsp olive oil

Directions:

- Heat olive oil in a pan over medium heat.
- Add garlic and onion to the pan and sauté until onion is softened.
- Transfer sautéed onion mixture to the soup maker.

- Add remaining ingredients to the soup maker and stir well.
- Cover soup maker with lid and cook on smooth mode.
- Serve and enjoy.

Nutritional Value (Amount per Serving):

- Calories 314
- Fat 4.4 g
- Carbohydrates 67 g
- Sugar 2.8 g
- Protein 3.9 g
- Cholesterol 0 mg

69-Flavorful Potato Soup

Time: 40 minutes

Serve: 4

Ingredients:

- 3 cups vegetable stock
- 14 oz can tomatoes, chopped
- 1 green pepper, chopped
- 1 tsp red chili flakes
- 1 tbsp tomato paste
- 1 tsp paprika
- 3 garlic cloves, minced
- 1 large onion, sliced
- 1 lb potatoes, diced

Directions:

- Add all ingredients to the soup maker.
- Cover soup maker with lid and cook on chunky mode.
- Serve and enjoy.

Nutritional Value (Amount per Serving):

- Calories 136
- Fat 1.8 g
- Carbohydrates 31.1 g
- Sugar 9 g
- Protein 3.9 g
- Cholesterol 0 mg

70-Simple Chicken Corn Soup

Time: 35 minutes

Serve: 4

Ingredients:

- 4 thyme stalks
- 1 tbsp parsley, chopped
- 2 ½ cups vegetable stock
- ½ cup sweet corn, drained
- 1 medium onion, chopped
- ¾ lb chicken breast, chopped
- 2 medium carrots, peeled and diced
- Pepper
- Salt

Directions:

- Add all ingredients to the soup maker.
- Cover soup maker with lid and cook on chunky mode.
- Season with pepper and salt.
- Serve and enjoy.

Nutritional Value (Amount per Serving):

- Calories 140
- Fat 2.9 g
- Carbohydrates 9.8 g
- Sugar 3.8 g
- Protein 19.2 g
- Cholesterol 54 mg

71-Mushroom Chicken Soup

Time: 30 minutes

Serve: 4

Ingredients:

- 1/2 cup cream
- 2 ½ cups vegetable stock
- 1 tbsp olive oil
- 1 tbsp parsley, chopped
- 1 medium onion, chopped
- 2 garlic cloves, sliced
- 1 large potato, peeled and cubed
- 1 cup mushrooms, sliced
- ¾ lb chicken, cooked and shredded
- Pepper
- Salt

Directions:

- Heat olive oil in a pan over medium heat.
- Add garlic and onion to the pan and sauté until onion is softened.
- Transfer sautéed onion mixture to the soup maker.
- Add remaining ingredients to the soup maker and stir well.
- Cover soup maker with lid and cook on smooth mode.
- Serve and enjoy.

Nutritional Value (Amount per Serving):

- Calories 272
- Fat 9.2 g
- Carbohydrates 22 g
- Sugar 4.1 g
- Protein 27.7 g
- Cholesterol 71 mg

72-Creamy Zucchini Soup

Time: 30 minutes

Serve: 4

Ingredients:

- 1 tsp fresh oregano, chopped
- 2 cups vegetable stock
- 2 garlic cloves, chopped
- 1 medium onion, chopped
- 1 ¾ lbs zucchini, chopped
- Pepper
- Salt

Directions:

- Add all ingredients to the soup maker and stir well.
- Cover soup maker with lid and cook on smooth mode.
- Season with pepper and salt.
- Serve hot and enjoy.

Nutritional Value (Amount per Serving):

- Calories 51
- Fat 1.4 g
- Carbohydrates 11 g
- Sugar 5.6 g
- Protein 2.8 g
- Cholesterol 0 mg

73-Zucchini Carrot Potato Soup

Time: 30 minutes

Serve: 6

Ingredients:

- 2 lbs zucchini, sliced
- 4 cups vegetable stock
- 1 tbsp butter
- 2 large carrots, diced
- 2 medium potatoes, diced
- 2 medium onion, chopped
- Pepper
- Salt

Directions:

- Melt butter in a pan over medium heat.
- Add onion to the pan sauté until softened.

- Add carrot, potato, and zucchini and sauté for 2 minutes.
- Transfer pan mixture to the soup maker.
- Add remaining ingredients to the soup maker.
- Cover soup maker with lid and cook smooth mode.
- Season with pepper and salt.
- Serve and enjoy.

Nutritional Value (Amount per Serving):

- Calories 121
- Fat 3.6 g
- Carbohydrates 23.3 g
- Sugar 7.5 g
- Protein 3.6 g
- Cholesterol 5 mg

74-Easy Cauliflower Soup

Time: 30 minutes

Serve: 2

Ingredients:

- 4 1/2 cups cauliflower florets
- 1 tbsp olive oil
- 2 cups leeks
- 1 cup water
- 2 cups vegetable stock
- 1 tsp salt

Directions:

- Add all ingredients to the soup maker and stir well.
- Cover soup maker with lid and cook on smooth mode.
- Season with pepper and salt.
- Serve warm and enjoy.

Nutritional Value (Amount per Serving):

- Calories 176
- Fat 8.5 g
- Carbohydrates 25.5 g
- Sugar 9.9 g
- Protein 5.8 g
- Cholesterol 0 mg

75-Anti-inflammatory Broccoli Ginger Soup

Time: 35 minutes

Serve: 6

Ingredients:

- 8 cups broccoli florets
- 2 tbsp ginger, chopped
- 4 cups leeks, chopped
- 2 tbsp butter
- 6 cups vegetable stock
- 1 tbsp olive oil
- 1 tsp turmeric
- 1/8 tsp black pepper
- 1 tsp salt

Directions:

- Melt butter in a pan over medium heat.
- Add leek to the pan and sauté for 5 minutes.
- Transfer sautéed leek to the soup maker.
- Add remaining ingredients and stir well.
- Cover soup maker with lid and cook on smooth mode.
- Serve warm and enjoy.

Nutritional Value (Amount per Serving):

- Calories 153
- Fat 9.3 g
- Carbohydrates 20 g
- Sugar 6.4 g
- Protein 4.5 g
- Cholesterol 11 mg

76-Lime Asparagus Cauliflower Soup

Time: 30 minutes

Serve: 2

Ingredients:

- 1 lb asparagus, cut into 1/2" pieces
- 1 cup cauliflower, chopped
- 1 large onion, chopped
- 3 cups vegetable stock
- 1 lemon juice
- 2 tbsp olive oil
- Pepper
- Salt

Directions:

- Heat oil in a pan over medium heat.
- Add onion and sauté until softened.
- Transfer sautéed onion to the soup maker.
- Add remaining ingredients to the soup maker.
- Cover soup maker with lid and cook on smooth mode.
- Season with pepper and salt.
- Serve warm and enjoy.

Nutritional Value (Amount per Serving):

- Calories 266
- Fat 16.5 g
- Carbohydrates 19.9 g
- Sugar 9.7 g
- Protein 14.1 g
- Cholesterol 0 mg

77-Flavorful Asparagus Soup

Time: 30 minutes

Serve: 4

Ingredients:

- 1 lb asparagus, ends trimmed and chopped
- 3 cups vegetable stock
- 2 garlic cloves, minced
- 1 large onion, diced
- 1 tsp lemon juice
- 1/2 cup coconut yogurt
- Pepper
- Salt

Directions:

- Add all ingredients to the soup maker and stir well.
- Cover soup maker with lid and cook on smooth mode.
- Season with pepper and salt.
- Serve warm and enjoy.

Nutritional Value (Amount per Serving):

- Calories 65
- Fat 0.7 g
- Carbohydrates 12.4 g
- Sugar 7.6 g
- Protein 3.5 g
- Cholesterol 0 mg

78-Spinach Broccoli Soup

Time: 30 minutes

Serve: 6

Ingredients:

- 2 1/2 cups broccoli florets
- 5 oz baby spinach
- 1 cup onion, chopped
- 4 1/2 cups vegetable stock
- 3 garlic cloves, minced
- 1/2 tsp black pepper
- 1 1/2 tsp salt

Directions:

- Add all ingredients to the soup maker and stir well.
- Cover soup maker with lid and cook on smooth mode.

- Season with pepper and salt.
- Serve warm and enjoy.

Nutritional Value (Amount per Serving):

- Calories 58
- Fat 1.3 g
- Carbohydrates 6.5 g
- Sugar 2.1 g
- Protein 5.7 g
- Cholesterol 0 mg

79-Healthy Bean Soup

Time: 35 minutes

Serve: 4

Ingredients:

- 1/2 cup dried lima beans, soaked overnight and drained
- 1 tbsp honey
- 1 tbsp lemon juice
- 2 tbsp fresh dill, chopped
- 3/4 cup tomatoes, chopped
- 3 cups vegetable stock
- 1 small onion, chopped
- 1/4 tsp pepper
- 1/4 tsp salt

Directions:

- Add all ingredients to the soup maker and stir well.
- Cover soup maker with lid and cook on chunky mode.
- Season with pepper and salt.
- Serve warm and enjoy.

Nutritional Value (Amount per Serving):

- Calories 60
- Fat 0.4 g
- Carbohydrates 13.2 g
- Protein 2.3 g
- Sugar 6.7 g
- Cholesterol 0 mg

80-Smooth Berry Apple Soup

Time: 30 minutes

Serve: 4

Ingredients:

- 2 apples, peeled, cored and sliced
- 2 cups water
- 2 cups apple juice
- 1 tbsp honey
- 1 tsp nutmeg
- ½ tsp cinnamon
- ½ tsp ginger
- ¾ lb cranberries
- 1 orange juice

Directions:

- Add all ingredients to the soup maker.
- Cover soup maker with lid and cook on smooth mode.
- Serve and enjoy.

Nutritional Value (Amount per Serving):

- Calories 191
- Fat 0.6 g
- Carbohydrates 44.4 g
- Sugar 33 g
- Protein 0.6 g
- Cholesterol 0 mg

81-Creamy Lentil Soup

Time: 30 minutes

Serve: 6

Ingredients:

- ½ cup red lentils, rinsed and soaked in water for 30 minutes
- ½ tsp ground cumin
- 3 cups vegetable stock
- 14 oz can tomatoes, crushed
- 1 onion, chopped
- 1 garlic clove, minced
- 2 large carrots, diced
- Pepper
- Salt

Directions:

- Add all ingredients to the soup maker.
- Cover soup maker with lid and cook on smooth mode.
- Season with pepper and salt.
- Serve warm and enjoy.

Nutritional Value (Amount per Serving):

- Calories 91
- Fat 0.6 g
- Carbohydrates 17.6 g
- Sugar 4.9 g
- Protein 5.2 g
- Cholesterol 0 mg

82-Basil Tomato Soup

Time: 30 minutes

Serve: 6

Ingredients:

- 2 ½ cups vegetable stock
- 2 tbsp basil pesto
- 1 garlic clove, minced
- 1 large potato, peeled and diced
- 1 medium onion, diced
- ½ bell pepper, diced
- 2 cans tomatoes
- Pepper
- Salt

Directions:

- Add all ingredients to the soup maker.
- Cover soup maker with lid and cook on smooth mode.
- Season with pepper and salt.
- Serve warm and enjoy.

Nutritional Value (Amount per Serving):

- Calories 74
- Fat 1 g
- Carbohydrates 16.7 g
- Sugar 2.6 g
- Protein 2.2 g
- Cholesterol 0 mg

83-Thai Chicken Soup

Time: 30 minutes

Serve: 4

Ingredients:

- 4 cups chicken stock
- 2 chicken breast, cooked and diced
- ½ cup spring onions, sliced
- 1 tbsp ginger, grated
- 1 garlic clove, minced
- 1 red chili, sliced
- 1 lime juice
- 2 tbsp curry paste

Directions:

- Add all ingredients to the soup maker.
- Cover soup maker with lid and cook on smooth mode.

- Season with pepper and salt.
- Serve and enjoy.

Nutritional Value (Amount per Serving):

- Calories 142
- Fat 6.5 g
- Carbohydrates 5 g
- Sugar 1.1 g
- Protein 15.2 g
- Cholesterol 37 mg

84-Bell Pepper Tomato Soup

Time: 30 minutes

Serve: 4

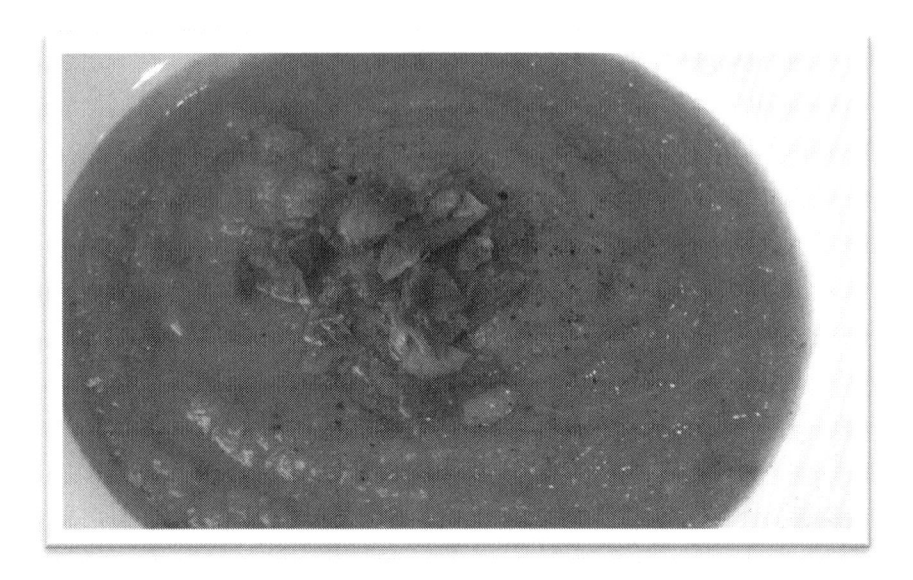

Ingredients:

- 2 chorizo sausages, diced and cooked
- ½ cup basil leaves
- ½ tsp red chili flakes
- ½ tsp ground cumin
- 1 tbsp olive oil
- 2 ½ cups vegetable stock
- 1 onion, diced
- 1 potato, diced
- 14 oz can tomatoes, diced
- 3 red bell peppers, diced

Directions:

- Add all ingredients to the soup maker.
- Cover soup maker with lid and cook on smooth mode.
- Season with pepper and salt.
- Serve and enjoy.

Nutritional Value (Amount per Serving):

- Calories 268
- Fat 16.6 g
- Carbohydrates 23.8 g
- Sugar 10.6 g
- Protein 10.3 g
- Cholesterol 26 mg

85-Spinach Coconut Soup

Time: 35 minutes

Serve: 4

Ingredients:

- 1 garlic clove, grated
- 2 cups fresh spinach, chopped
- 1 cup coconut milk
- 3 medium potatoes, peeled and diced
- 1 ½ cups water
- 1 ½ cups vegetable stock
- 1 tbsp ginger, minced
- 1 onion, chopped
- 1 tbsp olive oil
- Pepper
- Salt

Directions:

- Heat oil in a pan over medium heat.
- Add ginger, garlic, and onion to the pan and sauté until onion is softened
- Transfer sautéed onion mixture to the soup maker.
- Add remaining ingredients to the soup maker.
- Cover soup maker with lid and cook on smooth mode.
- Season with pepper and salt.
- Serve warm and enjoy.

Nutritional Value (Amount per Serving):

- Calories 302
- Fat 18.9 g
- Carbohydrates 33.5 g
- Sugar 5.9 g
- Protein 5 g
- Cholesterol 0 mg

86-Almond Broccoli Soup

Time: 30 minutes

Serve: 4

Ingredients:

- 4 cups vegetable stock
- 1 ½ lbs broccoli florets
- 3/8 cups ground almonds
- Pepper
- Salt

Directions:

- Add all ingredients to the soup maker.
- Cover soup maker with lid and cook on smooth mode.
- Season with pepper and salt.
- Serve and enjoy.

Nutritional Value (Amount per Serving):

- Calories 120
- Fat 7 g
- Carbohydrates 15.2 g
- Sugar 5.3 g
- Protein 6.6 g
- Cholesterol 0 mg

87-Beef Mushroom Soup

Time: 45 minutes

Serve: 4

Ingredients:

- ½ tsp thyme
- 3 ½ cups chicken stock
- ¾ lb beef strips, stir-fried
- 2 tbsp tomato puree
- 2/3 cup water
- 5 mushrooms, quartered
- 1 cup spinach
- 2 garlic cloves, sliced
- 1 onion, diced
- 1 tbsp olive oil

Directions:

- Heat oil in a pan over medium heat.
- Add garlic, onion, and spinach to the pan and sauté for 5 minutes.
- Transfer pan mixture to the soup maker.
- Add remaining ingredients to the soup maker and stir well.
- Cover soup maker with lid and cook on chunky mode.
- Season with pepper and salt.
- Serve and enjoy.

Nutritional Value (Amount per Serving):

- Calories 444
- Fat 33.4 g
- Carbohydrates 6.7 g
- Sugar 2.6 g
- Protein 28.7 g
- Cholesterol 101 mg

88-Chunky Onion Soup

Time: 45 minutes

Serve: 4

Ingredients:

- 1 thyme sprig
- 1 bay leaf
- 1 tbsp vinegar
- 3 cups vegetable stock
- 1 tbsp brown sugar
- 4 large onions, sliced
- 1 tbsp butter
- 1 tbsp olive oil
- Pepper
- Salt

Directions:

- Heat oil and butter in a pan over medium heat.
- Add sliced onion to the pan sauté until lightly golden brown.
- Transfer sautéed onion to the soup maker along with remaining ingredients and stir well.
- Cover soup maker with lid and cook on chunky mode.
- Season with pepper and salt.
- Serve and enjoy.

Nutritional Value (Amount per Serving):

- Calories 127
- Fat 7 g
- Carbohydrates 16.8 g
- Sugar 9.1 g
- Protein 1.7 g
- Cholesterol 8 mg

89-Potato Chickpea Soup

Time: 30 minutes

Serve: 4

Ingredients:

- 1 tbsp olive oil
- 2 garlic cloves, chopped
- 1 tbsp cumin seeds
- 3 cups vegetable stock
- ¼ cup parsley, chopped
- ¼ cup leek, chopped
- 1 sweet potato, diced
- 14 oz can chickpeas, drained
- Pepper
- Salt

Directions:

- Add all ingredients to the soup maker.
- Cover soup maker with lid and cook on smooth mode.
- Season with pepper and salt.
- Serve warm and enjoy.

Nutritional Value (Amount per Serving):

- Calories 194
- Fat 6.6 g
- Carbohydrates 32 g
- Sugar 3.7 g
- Protein 6.1 g
- Cholesterol 0 mg

90-Creamy Potato Leek Soup

Time: 30 minutes

Serve: 4

Ingredients:

- 1 vegetable stock cube
- 2 ¾ cups hot water
- ½ cup cream
- 1 large onion, chopped
- 2 cups leek, chopped
- 1 lb potatoes, peeled and chopped
- Pepper
- Salt

Directions:

- Add all ingredients to the soup maker.
- Cover soup maker with lid and cook on smooth mode.
- Season with pepper and salt.
- Serve and enjoy.

Nutritional Value (Amount per Serving):

- Calories 140
- Fat 2 g
- Carbohydrates 28.6 g
- Sugar 5.2 g
- Protein 3.2 g
- Cholesterol 6 mg

91-Paprika Pumpkin Soup

Time: 30 minutes

Serve: 4

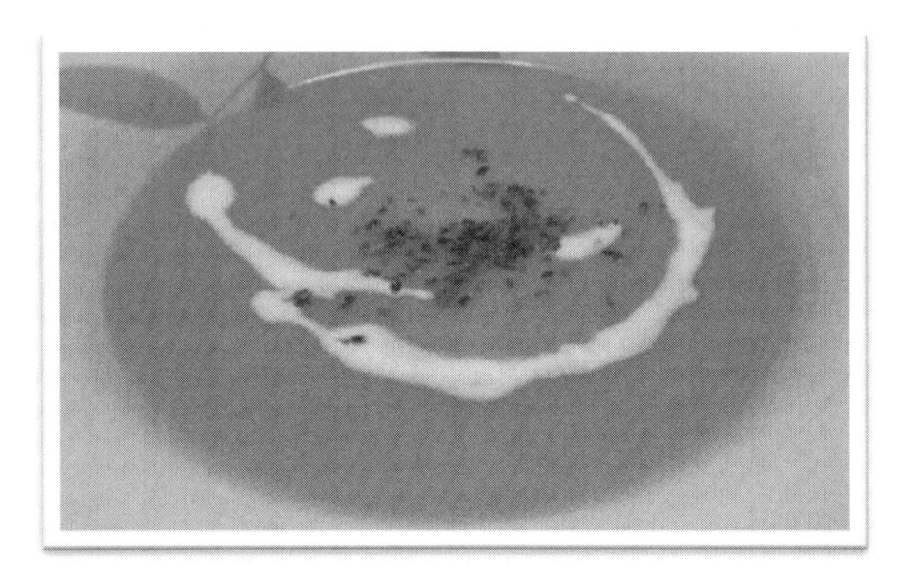

Ingredients:

- 1 tsp paprika
- 5 garlic cloves, minced
- 1 medium onion, chopped
- 1 tsp curry powder
- 4 cups water
- 2 cups pumpkin
- Pepper
- Salt

Directions:

- Add all ingredients to the soup maker.
- Cover soup maker with lid and cook on smooth mode.
- Season with pepper and salt.
- Serve warm and enjoy.

Nutritional Value (Amount per Serving):

- Calories 61
- Fat 0.5 g
- Carbohydrates 14.3 g
- Sugar 5.3 g
- Protein 2 g
- Cholesterol 0 mg

92-Autumn Bean Soup

Time: 30 minutes

Serve: 4

Ingredients:

- 2 ½ cups vegetable stock
- ¼ cup parsley, chopped
- 1 tbsp butter
- 1 medium potato, diced
- 1 small carrot, chopped
- 1 large onion, chopped
- 1 lb runner beans
- Pepper
- Salt

Directions:

- Melt butter in a pan over medium heat.
- Add onion to the pan sauté until onion is softened.
- Add runner beans and sauté for 2 minutes.
- Transfer onion-bean mixture to the soup maker.
- Add remaining ingredients to the soup maker.
- Cover soup maker with lid and cook on smooth mode.
- Season with pepper and salt.
- Serve and enjoy.

Nutritional Value (Amount per Serving):

- Calories 261
- Fat 4.3 g
- Carbohydrates 53.3 g
- Sugar 3.9 g
- Protein 10.4 g
- Cholesterol 8 mg

93-Avocado Zucchini Soup

Time: 30 minutes

Serve: 4

Ingredients:

- 2 tbsp fresh lemon juice
- ½ avocado, diced
- 2 tbsp mint leaves
- 3 ½ cups vegetable stock
- 1 ½ lb zucchini, chopped
- 1 garlic clove, minced
- 1 small onion, chopped
- 2 tbsp olive oil
- Pepper
- Salt

Directions:

- Heat oil in a pan over medium heat.
- Add garlic and onion to the pan and sauté until softened.
- Transfer sautéed onion to the soup maker.
- Add remaining ingredients to the soup maker and stir well.
- Cover soup maker with lid and cook on smooth mode.
- Serve and enjoy.

Nutritional Value (Amount per Serving):

- Calories 159
- Fat 14.1 g
- Carbohydrates 11.9 g
- Sugar 5.7 g
- Protein 2.9 g
- Cholesterol 0 mg

94-Green Bean Tomato Soup

Time: 40 minutes

Serve: 6

Ingredients:

- 3 cups fresh tomatoes, diced
- 1 lb green beans, cut into 1-inch pieces
- 1 cup carrots, chopped
- 1 cup onion, chopped
- 1 tsp basil, dried
- 1 garlic cloves, minced
- 6 cups vegetable broth
- 1/4 tsp pepper
- 1/2 tsp salt

Directions:

- Add all ingredients to the soup maker.
- Cover soup maker with lid and cook on chunky mode.
- Season with pepper and salt.
- Serve warm and enjoy.

Nutritional Value (Amount per Serving):

- Calories 94
- Fat 1.7 g
- Carbohydrates 13.6 g
- Sugar 5.9 g
- Protein 7.4 g
- Cholesterol 0 mg

95-Celery Soup

Time: 30 minutes

Serve: 4

Ingredients:

- 6 celery stalks, chopped
- 1 tsp chives, chopped
- 1 tsp mixed herbs
- 2 cups water
- 4 large carrots, chopped
- 1 large onion, chopped
- Pepper
- Salt

Directions:

- Add all ingredients to the soup maker.
- Cover soup maker with lid and cook for 25 minutes on blend mode.
- Season with pepper and salt.
- Serve and enjoy.

Nutritional Value (Amount per Serving):

- Calories 49
- Fat 0.1 g
- Carbohydrates 11.5 g
- Sugar 5.5 g
- Protein 1.2 g
- Cholesterol 0 mg

96-Chunky Veggie Soup

Time: 35 minutes

Serve: 2

Ingredients:

- 1 tbsp thyme
- 1 tsp garlic paste
- 1 tbsp tomato paste
- 1 vegetable stock cube
- 1 small turnip, chopped
- 1 cup cauliflower, chopped
- 2 large tomatoes, chopped
- ½ bell pepper, chopped
- 2 large carrots, chopped
- 1 ½ cups water
- Pepper
- Salt

Directions:

- Add all ingredients to the soup maker.
- Cover soup maker with lid and cook on chunky mode.
- Season with pepper and salt.
- Serve warm and enjoy.

Nutritional Value (Amount per Serving):

- Calories 105
- Fat 0.7 g
- Carbohydrates 23.9 g
- Sugar 13.2 g
- Protein 4.3 g
- Cholesterol 0 mg

97-Eggplant Asparagus Soup

Time: 30 minutes

Serve: 4

Ingredients:

- 2 tbsp tomato paste
- 2 vegetable stock cubes
- 1 medium onion, chopped
- 2 medium potatoes, peeled and chopped
- 2 eggplant, peeled and chopped
- ¾ lb asparagus, chopped
- Water
- Pepper
- Salt

Directions:

- Add all ingredients to the soup maker.
- Pour water into the soup maker up to the maximum mark.
- Cover soup maker with lid and cook on smooth mode.
- Season with pepper and salt.
- Serve warm and enjoy.

Nutritional Value (Amount per Serving):

- Calories 170
- Fat 0.9 g
- Carbohydrates 38.2 g
- Sugar 11.8 g
- Protein 6.7 g
- Cholesterol 0 mg

98-Creamy Eggplant Soup

Time: 30 minutes

Serve: 4

Ingredients:

- 3 cups hot water
- 1 cup fresh cream
- 1 tsp mixed herbs
- 1 vegetable stock cube
- 7 oz butter beans
- 1 lb eggplant, cut into cubes
- Pepper
- Salt

Directions:

- Add all ingredients to the soup maker.
- Cover soup maker with lid and cook on smooth mode.

- Season with pepper and salt.
- Serve and enjoy.

Nutritional Value (Amount per Serving):

- Calories 123
- Fat 4 g
- Carbohydrates 18.7 g
- Sugar 5.3 g
- Protein 5 g
- Cholesterol 11 mg

99-Sweetcorn Chicken Soup

Time: 30 minutes

Serve: 4

Ingredients:

- 1 tbsp butter
- 1 tbsp soy sauce
- ½ cup sweet corn
- 4 cups vegetable stock
- 1 tsp corn flour
- 1 tsp garlic paste
- 2 chicken breasts, cooked and shredded
- Pepper
- Salt

Directions:

- Add all ingredients except corn flour to the soup maker.
- Cover soup maker with lid and cook on smooth mode.
- Stir cornflour in 1 tbsp water and add in soup. Stir well.
- Season with pepper and salt.
- Serve warm and enjoy.

Nutritional Value (Amount per Serving):

- Calories 189
- Fat 9 g
- Carbohydrates 5.2 g
- Sugar 1.2 g
- Protein 22.1 g
- Cholesterol 73 mg

100-Chunky Zucchini Bean Soup

Time: 40 minutes

Serve: 4

Ingredients:

- 2 ½ cups vegetable stock
- 14 oz can tomatoes, diced
- 14 oz can red kidney beans, drained
- 5 green beans, chopped
- 1 medium zucchini, diced
- ½ tsp chili flakes
- 2 garlic cloves, minced
- 1 onion, diced
- 2 tbsp olive oil
- Pepper
- Salt

Directions:

- Add all ingredients to the soup maker and stir well.
- Cover soup maker with lid and cook on chunky mode.
- Season with pepper and salt.
- Serve and enjoy.

Nutritional Value (Amount per Serving):

- Calories 228
- Fat 8.9 g
- Carbohydrates 32 g
- Sugar 8.3 g
- Protein 8.7 g
- Cholesterol 0 mg

Conclusion:

What I like most about soup is how easy it is, both when cooking at home and eating out. The recipes in this book are easy and use familiar foods, so you can turn every day, easy-to-find ingredients into healthy diet friendly soup recipes that are delicious and full of the healthy fats your body will use to fuel itself. This book will walk you through everything you need to know about soup benefits and how to use your soup maker.

Printed in Great Britain
by Amazon

34908915R00125